JOEY DUNLOP

JOEY DUNLOP

HIS AUTHORISED BIOGRAPHY

MAC McDIARMID

Foreword by Bob McMillan

Haynes Publishing

First published in May 2001

A catalogue record for this book is
available from the British Library

ISBN 1 85960 822 1

Library of Congress catalog card no. 00-136556

Haynes North America Inc., 861 Lawrence Drive,
Newbury Park, California 91320, USA.

Published by Haynes Publishing, Sparkford,
Nr Yeovil, Somerset BA22 7JJ, UK.
Tel: 01963 442030 Fax: 01963 440001
Int.tel: +44 1963 442030 Fax: +44 1963 440001
E-mail: sales@haynes-manuals.co.uk
Web site: www.haynes.co.uk

Designed and typeset by G&M,
Raunds, Wellingborough, Northamptonshire
Printed and bound in Britain by
J.H. Haynes & Co. Ltd., Sparkford

Contents

Acknowledgements

Whatever their role in the life of Himself, I am deeply indebted to everyone who generously contributed their time and memories in the preparation of this book. In particular, I owe my gratitude to:

Joey's parents Willie and May Dunlop, his sisters Helen, Virginia and Margaret, and brothers Jim and Robert.

Bob McMillan, General Manager, Honda Racing UK, for writing the Foreword and giving such unstinting support at every stage of the project. His poem, and the poem by Donna Dunlop, both reproduced in the Endpiece, came very much from the heart.

Racers Roger Burnett, Mick Chatterton, Carl Fogarty, Mick Grant, Steve Hislop, Paul Iddon, Nick Jefferies, Eddie Laycock, Ian Lougher, Ray McCullough, Rob McElnea, Conor McGinn, Roger Marshall, Ian Switzer, Charlie Williams and Dave Woollams.

Peter Kneale, Chris Herring of Castrol Honda, Billy Nutt and Joe Wood, and race bosses Rex White and Barry Symmons.

Joey's former helpers, sponsors, technicians, mechanics and race-going friends, especially Slick Bass, Ernie Coates, Nick Goodison, Jackie and Sammy Graham, John Harris, Andy Inglis, Brendan McMullen, Marina Murphy, Bertie Payne, Merv 'Curly' Scott, John Smyth, and Davy Wood.

Rex Patterson and J.L. Snodgrass, both formerly of Ballymoney High School, Brian Kelly of the *Ballymoney Chronicle,* Robert Yarham of *Motocourse,* Norrie White, formerly of *Motor Cycle News,* and Samantha at *MCN* Archives.

The photographers who answered the call for their best images of Joey and whose work has added such a strong visual element to this story.

Darryl Reach and Flora Myer at Haynes Publishing – Darryl for doing so much to get the project rolling, Flora for her unswerving dedication to detail, and both for their enthusiasm and support.

And, above all, my very special and grateful thanks to Linda Dunlop and family.

Thank you all.

Foreword

by Bob McMillan, General Manager, Honda Racing UK

It's the stuff of fable, folklore and legend. In years to come this chronicle of a motorcycle racer's life will still be read with the same avid interest. Like the gladiators of old, Joey Dunlop gave us passion, pride, courage, danger and humanity all rolled into one.

I imagine people saying, 'Could that really happen, is that for real?' Is it possible that a poor, working class man could remain at the top of his chosen sport for over 31 years and in doing so stay in the hearts of race fans the world over? But not only race fans: he was adopted by thousands of Irish mothers, grand-mothers, granddads and children alike. Joey defied all the odds. I think like his legion of fans, he thought immortality to be his as he plied his trade over the decades.

To be honoured by politicians, press, public and royalty was the norm for 'Yer Maun'.

It gives an idea of Joey's stature that in 2001

Joey screams the Payne 250 Honda out of Waterworks on the way to winning the 1996 Lightweight TT. (Phil Masters)

Joey is congratulated by Sports Minister and compatriot Kate Hoey after his last Formula One win. Honda race boss Bob McMillan adds his congratulations. (Phil Masters)

Opposite: *Out on his own, The King of the Roads.* (Alastair McCook/Joey Dunlop Family Collection)

The mutual affection was clear. (Dave Collister)

he is to be posthumously awarded the Segrave Trophy, for the British subject who accomplishes the most outstanding demonstration of the possibilities of transport by land, air or water. The only other person to receive this award posthumously was Donald Campbell.

Alas the tale was to end in a far-flung place he loved to race in, where people also loved him – but only after fulfilling one more ambition. His Formula One TT win on the Honda VTR SP-1, followed with 125cc and 250cc wins that glorious week in June 2000, spoke volumes of the man.

'Too old', 'not strong enough', 'past it', 'waste of a good bike', 'won't even finish' – these are the words that linger in my mind from his doubters.

But if ever there was proof of one man's courage and fight against adversity, then the 226 miles of Formula One victory, at his fastest ever race speed, was it.

Mac McDiarmid's book tells the full story. Please read it, pass it on to your children and grandchildren and enjoy this tale of the world's greatest ever pure road racer – Joey Dunlop, a very special man.

Introduction

Joey Dunlop will be remembered as perhaps the greatest motorcycle road racer of all time. In total he won five world Formula One titles and more TT races than any other rider. In June 2000, at the unlikely age of 48, he added another three victories in the Isle of Man TT races, taking his tally to 26 – a dozen more than even the great Mike Hailwood.

Yet those who knew Joey best will remember 'The King of the Roads' as much for his manner off the track as his peerless performances on it. In an era in which sport and show business have fused into an almost seamless entity, Joey was a throwback to another age. Scornful of celebrity and indifferent to personal wealth, he raced, to use that old cliché, 'for the love of the sport'.

A devoted father of five, Joey was a devout and intensely private man. As a competitor he was generous of spirit, magnanimous in victory, and gracious in defeat, yet an ill-groomed public relations disaster with everyone but the people who really mattered – the fans.

One of seven children, he came from a poor background and 'didn't bother much with education'. Instead, he talked with his hands, whether racing a motorcycle at frightening speed, fettling his race-bikes or pulling a pint in his role as landlord of Joey's Bar, at Ballymoney, a small town in his native Northern Ireland.

Racing began 'as a bit of fun' in 1969, but it was to be 1976 before he was a regular winner of Irish races. In the same year he entered his first Isle of Man TT, finishing 16th in the 350cc

No place for doubt: hurtling flat-out over the crest at Rhencullen, 2000 TT. (Shane Ellis/Sportbike)

event. One year later, riding a 750cc Yamaha almost as unkempt as himself, he beat all the fancied riders to win the Jubilee TT.

In 1980 he scored his second TT win before beginning a fabulously successful relationship with Honda which lasted until his death. Like many of his compatriots, he specialised in racing on closed public roads rather than the relatively safe purpose-built circuits. As a rider he was not only blindingly quick but safe, precise and canny.

In 1986, in recognition of his racing success, Joey was awarded the MBE. A decade later, for a less publicised part of his life, he received the OBE, a tribute to his one-man relief trips to Romania and the Balkans. For Joey, dodging bullets to deliver blankets was the most natural thing in the world. Like much that he did, it was naïve but effective and came from the heart.

If he had never won a single motorcycle race

'Yer Maun', as he was known by thousands of adoring compatriots, would still have been an extraordinary Joe. Although he stopped smoking in 1995, my enduring memory of him is with a fag casually lodged in the corner of his mouth, smoke curling through long, lank hair, supping a pint with his mates and enjoying 'the craic'. That, and blasting a 750cc Honda along the TT course at speeds that left you breathless in disbelief.

It would be a gross exaggeration to say that I ever raced against Joey Dunlop, although I was sometimes on the same TT race track at the same time as the great man. Now and again, usually during practice, I'd catch a glimpse of him as he howled past, knees and elbows tucked tight in, carving fluent, effortless lines, and seemingly 50mph faster than me. Sometimes, I'd wonder why I bothered – before quickly realising that, even at my modest speeds, the buzz of TT racing was supremely addictive stuff. Joey Dunlop had that addiction more acutely than any other rider I can recall. Joey simply loved the TT course.

I first asked Joey to co-operate on a biography as long ago as 1996. His response was a definite 'maybe but not yet'. I got the clear sense that he saw such a book as some sort of full-stop on his racing career. Tragically, that is how it proved.

By the time this book is published, it will be almost one year since the unbelievable happened and Joey Dunlop died. But I imagine your shock is still intense. Mine certainly is, despite membership of perhaps the one group of people for whom 'Yer Maun' had little time: the media.

There is no journal of record for the life of William Joseph Dunlop. Other than the results of his races, there are few absolute truths about the man. Many of the chief witnesses to this account are Irish, and the Irish – if they can forgive me for suggesting as much – love a yarn. And if a little honest embellishment can improve a yarn, then so much the better.

Personally, I have no problem with that.

It's also true that many of the individuals who have generously given of their memories had too much to drink on at least some of the occasions they were endeavouring to recall. If that distorted reality a little, then in their defence one can only suggest that Joey would surely have wholeheartedly approved – if, indeed, he didn't sell or buy them the booze in question.

Then there are the journalistic sources, many from hacks on a deadline, many from scribblers who couldn't understand half of what the man said. So if they 'edited' his words here and there, that's only to be expected. Joey once cornered such an errant scribe with the words 'I couldn't have said it better meself, if I'd said it meself', which neatly sums up the point. Unless, of course, that tale is apocryphal too.

In other words I cannot claim that what follows is, entirely and without exception, the literal truth of Joey Dunlop's life. But those who knew him best tell me that it is an accurate reflection of a life that graced theirs, and mine – and, I hope, yours, too.

Gracious as ever, Joey acknowledges the cheers after winning his 25th TT. (Stephen Davison – Pacemaker)

Read all about it. (Stephen Davison – Pacemaker)

The Isle of Man TT

Road racing, the sport at which Joey Dunlop so excelled, is one of the oldest forms of motorcycle sport, and the Isle of Man TT races are its oldest surviving example. On 15 March 1904, after the British Government ruled out similar measures, the Tynwald (Manx Parliament) passed 'an Act to provide the authorisation of Races with Light Locomotives'.

Although there had been earlier Manx road races, on four wheels as well as two, the motorcycle TT dates from 1907 when Charlie Collier's Matchless won the Marquis de Mouzilly St. Mars Trophy and a princely £25.

Those early competitions were 'reliability trials' designed to test the durability of these new-fangled motorcycles, hence the expression Tourist Trophy. The 1907 TT was run over a 15.8-mile lowland course beginning near Tynwald Hill at St Johns. By 1911 the races had moved to a course running over a shoulder of Snaefell Mountain. The upland section was nothing more than a rutted track, and the first and last men through had to open and close livestock gates as they went. Even Bray Hill, today a sensational 150mph dive through suburban Douglas, was a hedge-lined dirt road. The first TT was won with a fastest lap of just 41mph. By 2000, the lap record had risen to over 125mph.

As racing developed, purpose-built circuits began to appear and these now host the predominant form of motorcycle speed sport.

Only in a few countries does public roads racing cling on, partly for reasons of tradition, partly because of the lack of funds to build closed road circuits. Other than the TT, the Formula One car grand prix at Monaco is perhaps the best-known example. In Irish parlance, racing is divided into 'the roads', which means public highways, and 'the shorts' – short circuits. With no less than a dozen regular public road venues, Ireland remains beyond question the world's road race centre.

To TT fans it's not the Isle of Man, but 'The Island' – capitalised, even in speech. More than that, it's 'Bikers' Island', as though the indigenous population were merely caretakers for the other 50 weeks of the year. For a typical TT, something like 40,000 race fans will swell the local population of 72,000, bringing with them around 13,000 motorcycles. Every boarding house, hotel and guest house is booked up months in advance.

Some of the dangers of racing on roads and streets normally used by ordinary traffic are obvious. No amount of straw bales can make houses, walls, trees, banks, lamp-posts and other street furniture safe when motorcycles roar past them at up to 180mph. Unlike modern short circuits with their generous run-

At Summerland for the presentation of the 2000 Formula One trophy – the first of three in an unforgettable week. (Paul Lindsay – Pacemaker)

TT classes

The earliest TT races had classes for just single- and multi-cylindered machines (with a controversial and short-lived regulation about pedal-assistance). Then 1911 brought the 'classic' classes of Senior (500cc) and Junior (350cc), with the Lightweight (250cc) class appearing in 1922. The Ultra-Lightweight 125cc class was added in 1951. All four classes were later shared with grand prix classes for pure racing machines.

Production racing on essentially street-legal bikes began in 1967, resuming in 1996 after a six-year lay-off. In 1995, with the demise of the 350cc class, the Junior became a race for 600cc modified production machines in what for the previous six years had been named the Supersport 600 TT.

The 'Formula' classes arrived after the TT lost its grand prix status in 1976. Initially there were three classes, although only Formula 1 remains. Initially limited to 1000cc machines, the capacity was reduced to 750cc in 1984. Both Senior and Formula 1 races are now open to the same machines, with a capacity limit of 1300cc, although separate lap records are kept for each class.

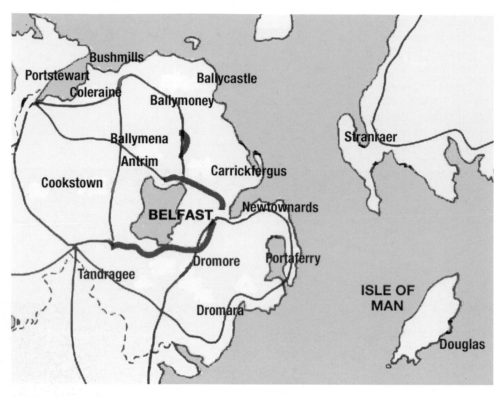

(courtesy Premier Print)

Where Joey lived, and where he loved to race.

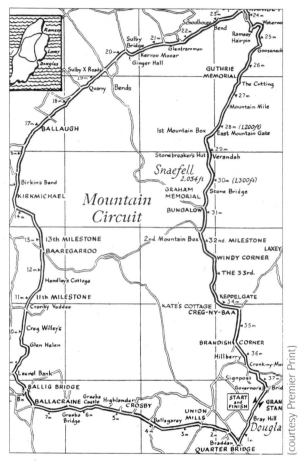

Opposite: Working on the 125 the day before his 26th and last TT win. (Mac McDiarmid)

off areas, here crashing is something riders can rarely afford. In the 94 years since racing began, the TT course alone has claimed something like 200 racers' lives.

There are subtler hazards too. Cambers and contours are far more complex than on short circuits and the surface itself will vary in terms of composition and grip. Overhanging trees and varying surface textures mean that sections dry out at different rates after rain. It will have more dust, gravel and general muck than any short circuit. Because of its sheer length, parts of the circuit may be wet while others are bone dry. Above all, it will have far more humps, ridges, lumps, bumps, leaps, dips and potholes.

To this you can add extreme length. At 37.73 miles the Mountain Course far exceeds any other race track in distance. Into those 37-odd miles the TT course packs something like 260 bends and kinks, each with its own particular problems and all potential killers. The course needs to be learned so thoroughly that, even at speeds close to 300 feet per second, it becomes second nature.

The speed at which the top racers tackle such hazards is awe-inspiring. Complex sequences of interlocking bends are knitted together at quite terrifying speeds, wheels skirting within inches of drystone walls, ditches and drains. And no-one did it more neatly than Joey Dunlop.

Joey's particular skill lay in plotting the line of least resistance through these myriad variables. He had a knack for finding the quickest line, the smoothest surface, the patches of road kindest to him and his machine. He was just as adept on small machines as on large ones. Make a small error on a 750cc racer and there's 150 horsepower on hand to bring the bike back onto the pace. Mess up on a 125cc racer, however, and that's a fast lap gone west. On the 'tiddlers', racers hoard speed more keenly than any miser ever clung to his gold.

Triple Triumphant

'It's strange. Everyone in the country feels they've lost a friend, whether they knew Joey or not.'
A motorcycle road racing fan

This was unthinkable. In 1999, for the first time anyone could remember – well, since 1981, anyway – not a single Irishman had won a race at the Isle of Man TT. Clearly something was out of kilter in road racing's natural order. Was this a shift in the scheme of things, or just a temporary aberration? Was the Irish bolt shot, or simply taking a year off? We had to wait only 12 months to find out.

The answer came on 3 June, in the first TT race of the new Millennium. On that Saturday afternoon the TT races witnessed something as close as such a fast and frenzied sport ever gets to a fairy-tale. After the fastest, most furious class of them all, a middle-aged man pulled his distinctive yellow crash helmet off his silver hair and grinned mightily. At the age of 48, and a dozen years after the last time, Joey Dunlop had won not just another Formula 1 TT, but a race he had never expected to win. Riding a factory-engined VTR-SP-1, and with former Honda President Mr Kawashima looking on, even Joey admitted to feeling under pressure in a race in which few gave him a realistic chance.

If conditions that day suited Joey better than anyone else in the field, that is only to say that he was also the field's most complete road racer. On a daunting mixture of wet and dry road Joey blasted into a lead he would relinquish only briefly throughout the six-lap race. For a moment during lap four the lead passed

to David Jefferies' R1 Yamaha before slick work by the Honda pit crew put Dunlop back ahead. Then, with conditions continuing to improve on lap five, the V&M machine's clutch basket exploded, sidelining last year's winner at Ballig Bridge. At the finish Dunlop led by almost a minute from Michael Rutter's Yamaha, with John McGuinness' SP-1 Honda a further 23 seconds behind in third.

Even before the finish, it was delirium. As Joey left the pits for his final stint, the grandstands stood and roared in exultation, and most of the other pit crews did too. Across the Glencrutchery Road, the cub scouts manning the antique scoreboard couldn't resist cheers and waves of their own. After the race, the finishing enclosure was more like a rugby scrum – if rugby is a game played by 2000 grinning souls.

Even the man himself seemed surprised by the emphatic nature of his victory, not to mention all the fuss. Sheer speed wasn't the issue so much as sustaining a high pace over six gruelling laps. 'I never thought I'd win another F1 race,' he admitted amidst emotional scenes, 'but I've never had a bike this good. It's the best bike I've ever ridden. I wondered during the week whether I could do six hard laps. We had some handling problems during practice and tried a load of different suspension settings, but it wasn't until we used the same tyre we used in last year's F1 race that it started coming together. On the final lap I eased off and I tried to be smooth.'

He may have been magnificent over the Mountain, but he struggled to open his 24th bottle of TT champagne. McGuinness and Rutter were in full spray by the time Joey opened his – and was left with the cork in his hand while the bottle ricocheted to the floor.

That night Joey did something even more unusual. At a private dinner attended by Mr Kawashima, Honda's very first racing boss, Joey plucked up as much courage as he'd needed for any of his TT wins. Putting his shyness to one side he actually made a little speech. 'I'd never seen him make one before,' remembers Honda team boss Bob McMillan. 'He'd just given Honda this amazing result, and stood up and thanked Mr Kawashima for help-

Looking more puckish than ever, Joey savours the victory plaudits at TT 2000 with his five children. (Stephen Davison – Pacemaker)

Opposite: *How close can you get? Joey hammers out of the Gooseneck, TT 2000.* (Stephen Davison – Pacemaker)

Flanked by Linda and Julie, Joey receives the Formula One trophy. (Stephen Davison – Pacemaker)

the roads of Ulster fully a quarter of a century before. Ensuring a proper degree of Irishness on the rostrum, Joey's younger brother Robert placed third. And for the third time in his career, Joey had a TT hat-trick under his arm.

Sadly, he will win no more. On 2 July 2000, just 25 days later, at an obscure race meeting near Tallin, Estonia, Joey Dunlop died instantly when he slid off that same 125cc Honda in the wet and hit a tree.

The motorcycle world was shocked to the marrow. But in Joey's native Ireland, the entire nation grieved, because here was one of those rare sportsmen who somehow transcended his own field. His funeral was broadcast live on national television, and attended by government ministers from Ulster, Westminster and Dublin. Some 50,000 mourners crammed the lanes around the little church at Garryduff, a mile from the Dunlop family home, along the same country road on which 'Yer Maun' had been known illicitly to test his racing bikes.

Following the funeral I bumped into a bloke in the bar at Belfast airport who said what many others were feeling. 'I'm not a motorcyclist but I loved Joey,' he admitted over a pint of Guinness, 'he was one of us.' Another Ulsterman, this time a keen bike racing fan, spoke of the extraordinary effect the loss had on the province: 'It's strange. Everyone in the country feels they've lost a friend, whether they knew Joey or not.'

He was that sort of guy. In an era in which sport, commerce and show business often fuse into a single money-grabbing entity, Joey was a throwback to another age. He raced because he loved to. In his own words, this generous, humble man 'never wanted to be a superstar. I just wanted to be myself and hope people remember me that way.' Those who knew him best will remember Joey as much for his nobility off the track as his exploits on it. That he was competing in an obscure race meeting in Estonia at all was testament to his creed that racing came first, with money so distant a second as to be almost invisible.

If racing on public roads is the oldest and 'purest' form of the sport, then Joey Dunlop's approach somehow made it purer still.

ing him get the bike.' It was a very special day.

People were still hugging themselves simply for being there as Joey had made history, when two days later he made a chunk more. On Monday 5 June, in his 25th year at the TT, he delivered up a quarter century of TT wins. In a rain-delayed Lightweight 250cc race, reduced from four laps to three, nothing could dampen the passion of the crowds as The King of the Roads put the youngsters in their place riding 'the best I've ever ridden The Island on a 250'. Could it possibly get better than this?

Well, this being a fairy-tale, of course it could. And it did – fittingly in racing's pixie class. Another two days into that breathless, heady week, Joey grabbed a TT win in the Ultra-Lightweight 125cc event. Fittingly, 16 seconds behind him was young Dennis McCullough – whose uncle Ray McCullough had been one of Joey's principal opponents on

Chapter Two

Windmills and Drainpipes

*'I was stood talking to Willie and this wee fella ran up, black from head to foot.
He wouldn't look you in the eye – just kept staring at his feet.
He'd been rebuilding a car engine and almost had it finished.
He'd have been about 10 at the time.'*

Jackie Graham of his cousin, the young Joey Dunlop

If there were any certainties about the future life of the young William Joseph, one was that somehow or other it would involve messing about with engines. His father, Willie, was a motor mechanic by trade and a practical if unconventional fixer by temperament. In the days before mains electricity was universal, he had once provided the family home with power by rigging a home-made windmill 65 'very scary' feet up in a nearby tree. When the North Antrim wind blew, the windmill turned the generator below and the Dunlop home glowed. It was Joe's job every night to check the batteries and if they were low, start up the generator. So it could be said that as far as motive power was concerned, Joe's first works contract was with the Almighty.

The future King of the Roads was born at 8.00am on 25 February 1952, possibly the one prompt Monday morning arrival of his life. Home at the time was a humble cottage without running water at Unchanaugh, a mile or so from the village of Dunloy. He weighed a healthy 7lb. Willie and May Dunlop would have seven children in all – four girls and three boys – of whom Joey was the eldest boy, 2½ years younger than big sister Helen. They were followed by Jim, Virginia and Linda. The last two children were

twins, Robert and Margaret, although one even younger child died of cot death aged six months. 'The wife did most of the bringing up', admitted Willie over a jar in the Ballymoney bar named after his son. 'I was busy earning money, and not much of that. We weren't the poorest family in the country, but not far off.'

They were hard times. Post-war rationing was still in force, and even for more affluent families, luxuries were scarce. As the windmill tale suggests, it was a time of improvisation and making the best of things. Perhaps spurred by necessity, Joey seems to have inherited his father's instinctive talent with machinery. The familiar name, however, came much later. 'All our children are known by their middle name,' explains Willie. 'Joey is William Joseph and Robert is Steven Robert. He was named after his Uncle Joe and when he was at school he insisted on that. He hated being called Joey. Wouldn't have it at all.'

Those who knew him best speak of the young Joe's even, somewhat reserved temperament and the same stubborn determination which would mark his race career. 'I only had to go to school because of him once,' remembers May, 'when he knocked a tin of black paint over another wee fella. But I don't think it was

deliberate. And as a wee'un he was good, even as a wee tote in a carry cot. He was a good sleeper – and he never lost that! And he was always a determined wee tote. He'd get into something and not let it go until he'd done with it. We used to cut a lot of turf, about 1½ miles from the house, and even when he was tiny he'd always insist on coming with us.'

There were just the usual childhood illnesses, and a propensity for bloody knees and noses that will surprise no-one familiar with Joe's later escapades. Both Unchanaugh, and later Bravallen Road, where the windmill stood and where brother Robert now lives, were quiet and out-of-the-way. Even when the opportunity arose, which was rarely, he wasn't one for 'running around with a crowd of people'.

The market town of Ballymoney – Ulster's best kept medium town of 1996 – was largely spared sectarian violence and not the worst of

places in which to grow up. For much of the time Joey's most available playmate was Helen, who would later marry Merv Robinson, mentor of his early racing career. Both children shared the Dunlop self-reliance, the same quiet ease in their own company. 'When mum was in hospital having the younger ones, me and Joey used to have to look after things,' explained Helen. 'But I like being on my own, just like he did. Maybe we both appreciated peace and quiet because we got so little of it at home. But the best time,' she adds in contradiction, 'was in our teens, when we were at the dances. Me mum used to send Joey with me to look after me, but it usually ended up the other way round. We'd get on the bus and go to Quay Road Hall in Ballycastle – the "in" place then – or The Strand in Portstewart ... see the Dave Clark Five, The Tremeloes, The Troggs ... although Joey wasn't really into music.'

Joey (No.1) racing the Tiger Cub at Maghaberry in 1969 or 1970. Bobby White leads. Number 18 is Joey's future manager, Davy Wood. (Davy Wood)

Opposite: A shy and youthful Joey captured in a publicity shot from 1981, the year he joined Honda Britain. (Don Morley)

A beaming Joey, circa 1976, with eldest child, Julie. (Joey Dunlop Family Collection)

his face. We tried to keep him away from mum until his eyebrows and hair grew back.'

Minor bangs and bloodshed were normal fare in an active household that didn't boast its first television until Joey was in his teens. 'We weren't spoilt as kids, because my mum and dad never had anything,' offers Robert, only for his wife Louise to say: 'They were all spoiled. Not with money – there was none – but indulged and supported in other ways.'

'In the evenings, when they were little,' May remembers, 'we'd either read them books or they'd play games around the fire. We were at Culduff before we got our first TV.'

'Aye,' agrees Willie, 'we took them out most Sundays, but not to the towns, because that cost money. We took them all over the north coast instead.' Whether it came from such family outings or elsewhere, Joey would never lose his fondness for Ireland's wilderness places, or his apparent indifference to creature comforts. Donegal would be a welcome if windswept bolt-hole even in the last month of his life.

Not surprisingly, formal tuition was not a trait in a family more at ease with hands-on learning or watching the real thing. Even more than most kids, Joe seemed to enjoy taking things to bits. 'I did quite a lot of work at home', explains Willie. 'There were always bits of engine lying around. That's probably where he picked some of it up.' Virginia is more certain. 'All I can remember him doing was working, out in the garage.'

Certainly books and blackboards were far less interesting than the cheery chaos at home. By all accounts young Joe didn't actually hate school, but he had no great use for it either. 'I didn't bother much with education', he once told me. Or as Willie puts it now, 'he wasn't good at learning'. Jenny Morrow, waitress at the High Street Café, Ballymoney, and a Joey fan like the rest of the town, remembers with a grin that the wee ragamuffin would 'get on the same school bus as me, but sometimes he'd get off again before it got there'. The cadets were a different matter however, perhaps because they did practical things, out of doors. For a while young Joe nursed ambitions of joining the army.

Earlier Helen had been responsible for breaking Joe's nose. 'It was an accident – I pulled a tractor harrow on top of him. There was a lot of blood – he always took terrible bloody noses. He was accident prone ... always falling off roofs and things like that. He once threw a load of paraffin in the stove and burnt

Brian Kelly, now editor of the *Ballymoney Chronicle*, was another contemporary of Joe at Ballymoney High School. 'He was an unassuming wee, thin fella with long hair. He was a bit mischievous, but I never remember him fighting or falling out. But I never remember him talking about bikes either – isn't that strange?'

J.L. Snodgrass, now retired, taught half of Ballymoney at the High School on the same Garryduff Road where Joey lived and was buried in July 2000. Remembered by Robert for his knack of 'lifting you up by the sideburns', Snodgrass perhaps performed the same service for young Joe, although the lad was not memorably badly behaved: 'I remember him, but he didn't really stand out. But in recent years I was pleased that he never forgot his roots in North Antrim. His feet were firmly on the ground, even if his wheels weren't always.'

The same anonymity cloaks the recollections of former headmaster Rex Patterson of the boy who was to become his school's most celebrated pupil. 'I have to say he made a much deeper impact after he left than whenever he was there.' In a voice cracking with emotion, he described the time Joey came to the school as a special guest on sports day. 'I introduced him as "the World Champion, our most distinguished past pupil". When I brought him up on to the stage, the applause lasted for 15 minutes – I have never seen anything like it.'

It's not hard to imagine Joey stood there now, shuffling his feet and smiling with embarrassment at the plaudits, just as he would when handed some huge TT trophy at the Villa Marina on the Isle of Man. Jackie Graham, later to become his mechanic, recollects: 'Even when he was a nipper he was a wee, shy thing. Didn't like at all to meet strangers.'

Of course the time would come when there were no such things as strangers, at least in Ballymoney. In fact it's hardly possible now to pause anywhere in town without chatting about Himself, what a fine man he was, a credit to the place and all, but mind you he was an awfully quiet fella too. Didn't have much to say …

This reticence would later cause the teenage girl who became his wife certain problems. 'We lived on the same estate, Hillcrest Gardens at Killyrammer,' explains Linda Dunlop. 'He lived up the avenue, I lived down. Killyrammer was about three miles from Ballymoney. It was a small, quiet place, just one housing estate here and one there, and not a shop between them.

'I was 15, he'd have been 16. He was quite shy then too and I had taken a wee fancy to him. I used to pass notes through his sister Linda. He wouldn't come down the avenue much, I had to go up to him. I must have been 16 when we started going out. He had long hair … looked rougher then … but very quiet.'

He may have been shy, but there were also signs that he could be wilful and persistent, qualities that would later mark his racing career. Another friend from the time recalls a

Young Joe eyes Ray McCullough during 1977, the year he truly reached the same level as the master of Irish racing. (David Wallace)

youthful Joey clambering up a drainpipe to see Linda, visits to which the neighbour's wife took gossipy exception. Joey didn't yell or remonstrate. That wasn't his style. Instead he simply clambered a little higher on his next visit, blocked their chimney with sods and filled the house with smoke.

Linda's mother, by all accounts, wasn't instantly impressed by her daughter's suitor, who not only shinned up the side of her house on a regular basis but, worse still, sported long hair at a time when there was no surer sure sign of dishonourable intent. It can't have helped when he was arrested and taken to court for the smoke stunt. 'But the judge just laughed', remembers May, 'said it was a silly prank. So he got off with a caution.'

For a young man in rural Ireland there are other ways to get your kicks. Although there was no history of racing in the Dunlop family, Ulster itself is steeped in the stuff. So it wasn't long before Merv, Helen's husband, talked Joey into taking his first tentative racing steps. Since Merv's own career as a speed demon was fleeting and impoverished, this amounted to less than factory support. If anything, Joey, earning around £2.00 per week 'washing engines' for his Uncle Dick Barclay's haulage firm, had even less money than Merv. Still, it would surely be a laugh.

It was evening in Joey's Bar, Ballymoney, one day in November 2000.

'Everyone says he started in '69, but I'd say '68,' reckoned Willie Dunlop.

'I think he did a meeting or two, then stopped and started the next year,' observed Andy Inglis.

'I remember he didn't have a car licence, so he gave his sister's licence number to the Union to get his race licence,' said Willie to his pint.

'Aye, Joey was very good with dates – better than the rest of us,' added Andy with a sigh.

That much, anyway, is true.

Like many of those who would become Joey's entourage, Andy of the silver hair and ruddy, smiling face, wishes he could remember it all just a little better. But even those who can aren't all that sure.

Brendan McMullen had become firm friends with Joey and Merv since meeting them potato-picking for Sam Bartlett three years before, and for a time worked with Joey at Dick Barclay's. Although he had no racing ambitions of his own, Brendan happened to have a 50cc Itom racer which Robo, as Merv was known to his mates, asked to borrow for a meeting at Lurgan Park in 1968. 'As it turned out,' he explains, 'it had a hand gearchange and he tried to convert it to foot-change but couldn't get it to work. But we all three of us went to watch anyway.' As far as anyone can tell, spectating at Lurgan Park that day was Joey's first taste of motorcycle racing.

As to actually competing, Joey himself once told me that he began racing in 1969, at Maghaberry, riding a Triumph Tiger Cub bought with £50 of borrowed money. Ivan Davison, road race convener to the Ulster centre of the MCUI, also believes Maghaberry was the place. A Maghaberry programme certainly exists from April 1969 listing J Dunlop amongst the entries. Yet Brendan is '1000 per cent sure' that the meeting in question was at Kirkistown on Easter Monday 1969, and he should know because he helped pay for the bike. He thinks Joey finished 'about sixteenth'. The Tiger Cub was a simple 199cc push-rod single developing perhaps 10 horsepower. Although scarcely a device for giving anyone a taste for genuine speed, it had enough about it to get the young Dunlop hooked.

The Motor Cycle Road Racing Club of Ireland ran three meetings that year at Maghaberry, a former military airfield that would later become a prison. In the first two meetings, the 200cc event was won by Ray McCullough, already a star and destined to become Joey's foremost rival in the mid-Seventies. Joey himself failed to figure in the top six, and it would be another two years before he'd reach such giddy heights. In one of those races, on board another Cub, was Davy Wood, who would later become Joey's unofficial manager: 'It was around June. All I can remember is that we both finished. The stars were long gone.'

I remember we both finished the race – but the stars were long gone

Joey leaps the 500 Yamaha in typical Irish road racing style. (David Wallace)

Merv Robinson's own career had begun, according to Brendan, with 'just one or two meetings in 1967 on a 197cc Villiers borrowed from Frank Kennedy. In 1968 he built a 175 Bantam. He was a good engineer and it was a really special machine, with a one-off frame made from Reynolds 531 tubing, disc-valve induction and driving through a Tiger Cub gearbox. But he only raced it about twice that year, and once in 1969, then swapped me for the Tiger Cub. Its first meeting was at Temple.'

If the start of both men's career was downbeat, the reason was as much poor equipment as slow-burning talent. When Robo acquired his own Tiger Cub, their budget was so feeble and spare parts so scarce that, as Helen remembers, 'they were struggling to qualify. Often they had to go in different heats because they didn't have enough parts to make two complete bikes, so they had to swap some bits over.' With only one serviceable machine between them, whichever qualified better got to race.

But though he may have lacked for parts,

support was a constant. 'Joey was always very close to his dad,' explains Linda, 'and took him to the races every weekend. His dad played a big part in his life.' In those early days, fettling the machine was initially down to Willie, who recalls his first faltering attempts at tuning for speed. 'We skimmed the head to raise the compression, and bolted on a different carb. We ended up building up the piston crown with weld, then Robo machined it down on his lathe. It was good for 100mph, downhill at Mid Antrim.'

Jackie Graham, shortly to join the Dunlop entourage, remembers the Triumph as 'a pretty rough thing, with bits and pieces welded to it where the frame broke, and a footrest. It was a fairly tatty wee bike. Joey had a Mini Traveller. To get to meetings he'd take the wheels out of the bike and shove it in the back.' But there were signs of the loner then too. 'You weren't always sure Joey wanted you there in those days. He didn't want you seeing him make a mess of it. So he and his father tended to sneak away to the races.'

Cookstown, 1977, front row, left to right: Steve Cull, Ray McCullough, Courtney Junk, and Joey. Merv Robinson is number 6 on the second row. (David Wallace)

Far from being the emerging road racer, 'his early races were on the shorts,' says Linda, 'Aghadowey, about five miles from here, and Bishopscourt. Och it was just a bit of fun. We didn't take it seriously – it was just one big friendly family having fun. But he always put his all into it, even when we had nothing. He never gave up, even if people were laughing at him. They were very poor days, Minis and trailers, doing without to pay for the bikes. There was no sponsorship.'

Support was mounting, however, as more friends and family joined in what was still as much a social as a competitive pursuit. Sister Virginia, six years Joey's junior, was a fiercely loyal member of this growing army who came close to fist-fighting rival fans at Temple one year. Not that there was much of a reputation to defend initially. 'I remember early on at Kirkistown when Brian Steenson and Cecil Crawford came first and second,' she chuckles, 'and we had to wait about 15 minutes for Joey and Merv to appear. It seemed like forever – like two different races. But we loved it. Until our kids arrived, we'd go to the races every weekend.'

The trade-mark yellow helmet had also yet to appear. Joey raced initially wearing a primitive pudding-basin lid with an ivy leaf motif on the front, in tribute to his hero, the late Bill Ivy. Brendan McMullen remembers it well: 'It was silver grey, and we were up until about 4.00 trying to draw that ivy. In the end we used a sycamore leaf as a pattern. You have to remember that Merv was a big Phil Read fan, so that made for a bit of fun between the two of them.' In the mid-Sixties, there was no greater racing rivalry than that between Yamaha team-mates Ivy and Read.

A bright yellow open-face 'jet' design helmet followed in 1971. The first full-face was a yellow Boeri donated by John Boyd, a Suzuki dealer from Ballymena. Although some friends recall that this had a seam down the middle which was covered with tape, contemporary photographs clearly show the stripes to be factory applied. Whatever its graphics, it was 'a really sloppy fit – he had to put some extra foam inside to stop it wobbling about'. The first

of several Kangol lids seems to have appeared in 1978, initially plain yellow but with a black stripe from 1979. In March 1982 Joey signed with Top Tek (Kangol's successor), before donning the familiar Arai in 1983.

Joey's first road race, also on the Triumph, came at the Temple 100 in 1970, riding number 32 in the 200cc handicap event. His earliest surviving trophy, a small, slightly battered silver metal cup, sits on a table in the sitting room. The engraving reads: 'Mid Antrim 5th place 1972 200cc class.'

In the room next door in the house on Garryduff Road, a couple of miles outside Ballymoney, are later, loftier spoils. Five FIM plaques, awarded for Joey's World Formula One titles, grace the left-hand wall, along with an *Irish Post* Special Millennium Award for Sport. On the dining table is daughter Donna's half-finished jigsaw puzzle of the Southern 100 races, her father's unmistakable yellow helmet centre picture. The spiral staircase to the upper floor was inspired by one in the hotel at Belgium's Zolder circuit, where dad clinched his third world title in 1984. Between that modest battered cup and the jigsaw lies the greatest career that motorcycle road racing has ever seen.

Willie Dunlop – Joey's most devoted supporter from Day One – looks on as his son prepares at Carrowdore in 1998. (Alastair McCook)

The Black Gurk

'I have to win the race because the rent's due.'
Joey Dunlop

*Curly Scott looks on as the Black Gurk
lines up for the North-West 200 in 1976.*
(Gavan Caldwell – Pacemaker)

Most racing seasons begin on a wave of optimism, but Joey's second season quickly turned sour. His sister Helen remembers the 1970 Easter Monday well: 'We were coming home from Kirkistown in the Mini, Joey and Linda in front, me and Merv in the back, and a trailer behind. Suddenly there was this big bang, and a car landed in the road in front of us – just like in that Volkswagen TV ad. It hadn't seen us slow down, hit the trailer and flown clean over the top of us. Our toolbox went through the windscreen of an on-coming car. Luckily no-one was badly hurt.' The damage, however, crippled Joey's already tenuous income, severely restricting his racing that year.

By 1971 the Tiger Cub had given way to another roadster-based machine, a Suzuki Invader. Whilst not exactly a cutting edge racer, the air-cooled 200cc two-stroke twin was appreciably more potent than the Triumph it had replaced. Rounding off the race preparation nicely was a new seat cover, run up in imitation leather by Jackie Graham's missus. Thus equipped, Joey scored a fourth place at Kirkistown on 12 April 1971, and a second at Tandragee two months later – his first rostrum finish.

'It had been raced and tuned in England,' Jackie recalls, 'I think by Faron, and we tuned it some more. We got it going fairly well. I put reed valves into it, and it would rev to 14,000, but the reeds would never last a race at that. You couldn't get decent racing pistons then. But it was a super wee engine, and stood a lot of abuse.'

This was just as well since large measures of abuse were what it got. By the standards of future factory HRC Hondas the engine work was crude, but sometimes surprisingly effective. Willie tells of that day at Tandragee when the Suzuki refused to start despite all their pushing. With their enthusiasm to get it running, fuel drained into the cylinders and hydraulic pressure bent a con-rod. Conventional mechanical wisdom would have seen them pack up and go home, but a man who builds windmills is not so easily beaten. 'I took off the barrel,' said Willie with an echo of his old defiance, 'wedged the rod with a tyre lever and thumped it with a stone. That got it straight enough to run. Joey came second in the race.'

Was he thinking, then, that on this evidence his son might be good?

'No, I thought he was mad. I told him to go easy. I was always thinking how much it would cost to fix if he fell off or blew up the bike.'

By now Joey had quite a racing entourage. As well as his wife, family, father, Jackie Graham and anyone else who cared to tag along, this included mechanic Mervyn 'Curly' Scott and storeman and general factotum, Andy Inglis. The arrival of another Mervyn, albeit one answering to 'Curly', seems also to have caused the original Merv to become known as 'Robo'.

1972

Curly had known Joey since the Tiger Cub days. 'He was working for his Uncle Dick in his haulage company when he got the 200 Suzuki, and I was working for Danny McCook. It was around 1972, and I'd broken my leg at the

The great Ray McCullough, Joey's predecessor as 'King of the Roads' and the captain of the Dromara Destroyers. (Clifford McLean – Pacemaker/ David Wallace)

Ray McCullough and Joey, dogfighting at Temple. 'Madness ... I'll never ride like that again' said the great man Ray. (Clifford McLean)

Merv Robinson, all smiles after winning the 500cc race at the 1975 Ulster Grand Prix. (Clifford McLean)

North-West 200. I wasn't racing – Tom Herron crashed and hit me on the left-hander at the top of Juniper Hill.'

Herron would be killed on the same hill in 1979, but Curly laughs as he recalls the aftermath to his broken limb. 'There were 22 racers in hospital – including Paul Smart, Tony Rutter, Tommy Robb – and I made 23. By this time Joey was driving lorries for Danny, and while I was injured he moved into my job in the workshop. When I was fit I started helping him out.'

At the time Danny McCook ran a coal merchant and hauliers yard located 100 yards or so from where Joey's Bar now stands. Initially, Joey was engaged in the coal side of the operation. Naturally, he had little difficulty attracting the customary veneer of that trade, earning the nickname of the 'Black Gurk'. Previously, Robo had been known as plain 'Gurk', a title he was evidently glad to dress up just a little and pass on to his brother-in-law. Although there is such a word in old Irish, no-one in Ballymoney now seems to know what a gurk of any hue might be, but the name stuck to Joey nonetheless.

Names weren't the only thing Robo was free with. 'He should have been fitted with horns,' Andy Inglis says with a grin. 'He was a real devil ... forever playing tricks on everyone. When the two Mervyns got together you had to look out. But he was a bit of a father figure to Joey – used to give him tips on how to make his bike faster. Joey would ignore whatever he said, beat him, then thank him for the advice.' But when he wasn't playing pranks, Robo would look out for Joey. At one of their early meetings he suggested to local photographer Gavan Caldwell that he take Joey's picture. Gavan, who'd no idea who Joey was, much less what he would become, took one look at 'this oily rag with long hair' and decided to save his film for something better. Naturally he now wishes he hadn't.

Joey and Linda were married on 22 September 1972 at a quiet ceremony at Ballymoney register office. Linda's brother-in-law was best man. The young couple – Linda was 19, Joey a year older – caught the Larne-Stranraer ferry that same afternoon, spending the next two weeks touring 'all over Scotland'. After a further two weeks living under Linda's mother's roof, they set up home at Bushside, a village two miles from Armoy.

At this time Frank Kennedy, who lived in Armoy and would later join forces with Joey and Robo, was racing a 344cc Aermacchi. Joey soldiered through the season with the Suzuki twin, whilst Robo was now riding Hugh O'Kane's AJS 7R. Joey's results were less than startling, but creditable enough to attract the attention of Danny McCook, who resolved to offer some much-needed help for the following year. Although Robo, too, was by then on a 'Macchi, Joey's was not ready in time for the first meeting, on which he posted sixth on the tired old Suzuki.

Jackie remembers the 'Macchi as 'a fairly good bike' and Joey as 'brilliant at getting the best out of it', but the Italian four-stroke single was no match for the screaming air-cooled Yamaha twins ridden by the likes of Tom Herron. So Merv and Joey spent much of the season dicing with each other for the minor places. Taking on Ireland's two most prestigious race meetings, the North-West 200 and the Ulster Grand Prix, was always likely to be ambitious. Joey's first North-West entry became a disaster when the final drive chain snapped at the start. Three months later his maiden Ulster Grand Prix was slightly more satisfactory. Riding against the likes of Mick Grant, Charlie and John Williams for the first time, he placed 19th on the first four-stroke home.

1974

By this time Joey and Robo's racing calendar was bulging. From the early days until Julie was born in 1974, Linda threw herself into this increasingly bike-dominated lifestyle without question: 'I remember those days all right. We were away every week ... Maghaberry ... Kirkistown ... St Angelo ... Mondello Park ... I never missed any races in the early days.'

This was more than could be said for Robo and Joey. Helen recalls: 'When Joey fell off once at St Angelo [near Enniskillen], me and

Linda piled into the ambulance with him. We were both pregnant, so the crew were more worried about us than Joey.

'At the time Merv and Joey only had one bike between them, so Merv must have thought his luck was in when Joey fell off – it meant he definitely got a race. At the hospital we were

Frank (left) and Merv ponder the Yamaha's engine, 1977. (David Wallace)

Merv and Joey preparing for the off at Cookstown in 1977, and already surrounded by helpers and fans. (David Wallace)

sat with Joey after they said he'd broken his collarbone, and who do we see being wheeled past on a stretcher but Merv?'

At the final open meeting at Maghaberry, Merv and Joey – recently recovered from yet another snapped collarbone – contested three races on Aermacchis. Merv beat Joey each time, with a best place of second to Joey's third. Later, in a closed meeting, Gordon Bell's Yamaha, then sponsored by John Rea, was 'pushed all the way' as Joey hustled to second place. It wouldn't be the last time Joey impressed the Rea brothers. The season also included Joey's first visit to the Isle of Man, to a club meeting at Jurby. If a second and two third places was encouraging, events would prove that his chosen means of transport to The Island – a fishing boat – was not.

In 1974 the racing began to get serious, with the first in a succession of Yamahas, an air-cooled 350cc twin bought by Danny McCook. Willie remembers that even getting the bike was an adventure, since Danny's van was searched at Stranraer on his way to collect it. Customs officials were so interested in the £2000 in cash earmarked for the purchase that they quite failed to notice that the van was full of red diesel.

On a competitive machine at last, Joey started to get results, beginning with a third place at Kirkistown. At the first Maghaberry meeting, Merv beat Joey into second. Next time out Merv retired when his exhaust came adrift, gifting Joey the win.

Jackie Graham remembers the Yamaha as '... yellow, you could always see it coming. It was a fairly quick bike, at least for two or three laps. Then, like most air-cooled engines, it slowed as it overheated. We had a lot of trouble with pistons cracking, but didn't have the money to put new ones in as often as we should. Once we were at Frank's, going through a box of used water-cooled pistons for the ones with the least cracks, then modifying them to suit the air-cooled engine. Joey told me that if he didn't make 'a pound or two' that year, he was stopping. He was very conscious that Linda didn't have a washing machine and lots of things other wives had.'

Even when he began winning, the pickings were slim. 'Maybe £20 or £30 for a win – not very much for risking your neck', as Joey observed at a time when a new TZ racer plus spares kit cost around £3500. It was a struggle, but there were high points, notably at Mondello Park. 'When he beat John Rea's rider Gordon Bell on the liquid-cooled bike, that made him sit up and take notice,' says Jackie Graham.

And not only potential sponsors were paying attention. There's always been a degree of tribalism to Irish racing which sometimes attracts the sort of partisan support that football does elsewhere. Success meant that both Joey and Merv were beginning to attract their followers. Inevitably, after a few post-race bevvies, rivalries could boil over. Jackie remembers at least one brawl between Joey's fans and supporters of the rival Bell brothers. Not that Joey himself was a fighter. 'Only once have I known him to scrap,' insists Jackie's son, Sammy. 'Someone was misbehaving in the bar once and wouldn't stop, so Joey picked up a pool cue, thumped him, and out he went.'

1975

In 1975 the Rea brothers – John, Martin, Noel and their company, Rea Distribution – stepped

in as sponsors with another 350 Yamaha. The season got off to a flying start at Croft, near Darlington, with a third place behind Kork Ballington – later to become World Champion – and Roger Marshall. Back in Ireland, other eye-catching performances followed, notably double wins at Mondello Park and St Angelo.

Merv Robinson getting in a spot of illegal testing on his 350 TZ Yamaha. Joey is riding the other bike. (David Wallace)

Joey on the 350 Rea Yamaha in around 1978. The old green leathers have been re-sleeved. (David Wallace)

Merv's bike, hooked up to his Rover. Race transporters have come on since. (David Wallace)

Opposite: *Sponsorship from John Rea helped Joey make the breakthrough from midfield to rostrum rider.* (Clifford McLean – Pacemaker)

Merv in happy mood. His death at the 1980 North-West 200 affected Joey deeply. (David Wallace)

Perhaps most significant of all, Joey was beginning to give the top Irish rider of the period, Ray McCullough, serious bother in straight head-to-head fights. At the Ulster Grand Prix, McCullough regularly beat the best in the world, and by some margin. In 1971, the last year the Dundrod event was a World Championship round, he had led the great Jarno Saarinen home by no less than 1½ minutes.

Joey wasn't quite in that class yet, but he was becoming one of the names of Irish racing, although many thought Merv still had the edge. 'Joey and Robo used to egg each other on,' remembers Curly. 'In the early days everyone reckoned Merv was better, although I don't think Joey thought so. They used to race to Armoy on the road – Joey on his C15, Merv on a Villiers-engined Sun – and Joey reckoned he could always stick with Merv.'

Curly, up to his elbows in pistons and crankshafts, remembers 1975 differently. The 350 spent the season 'forever seizing – we never did fix that – but it actually finished at Tandragee, in second, behind Ray McCullough. In fact Ray was one of the people who'd suggested that John Rea support Joey. After that John was sold on Joey. He decided he needed better bikes, and bought a new TZ350 and a Seeley frame.' As well as being stiffer than the standard Yamaha chassis, the Seeley was longer and much more stable over the ferociously bumpy road circuits in which Ireland specialised. To help the bikes ride the bumps better still, Willie would later lay down the twin rear shock absorbers to give more rear wheel travel.

The relationship between John and Joey was one of respect and affection as much as the usual marriage of convenience between sponsor and racer. Many years later Linda would describe John Rea as 'very, very good, like a second father to Joey, right up to the time Honda snapped him up'. But for the moment what her man needed most of all was reliable equipment.

Faced with seizures in important races at the North-West 200, Cookstown and elsewhere, but seeing enough to know their man was on his

Merv and Joey share a joke before another battle on the Ulster lanes. (David Wallace)

way, the Rea brothers lashed out on more machinery. Armed with a new 350 Yamsel, Joey took the 'King of Kirkistown' title first time out. Major wins that year included the Temple 100, Leinster 200 and Carrowdore 100.

Curly recalls that 'somehow Joey ended up with three bikes – 250, 350 and a 351cc '500' – all with Seeley frames. He also put a Seeley frame in the first four he got, an ex-Pat Mahoney 700 Yamaha. I'd take two bikes home with me to work on, Joey would take two home with him, and we'd swap them the following week. It was a very exciting time – and very time-consuming. Sometimes we'd get home on

Tuesday and be off again on Thursday.'

It was around this time that Joey began to be noticed by UK riders trying their hand on the Irish roads. Roger Marshall, later his Honda team-mate, remembers Joey first from visiting the 1975 Ulster GP with Phil Haslam and Steve Machin. 'I got to like the bloke later, so I don't want to criticise, but to be frank he looked like a coalman. But you could tell even then that he could ride. In fact I have two outstanding memories of road racing. One is breaking down at Windy Corner and watching Hailwood win that fabulous race in 1978. The other is Joey almost anywhere – phenomenal, inch perfect.'

Chapter Four

The Armoy Armada

*'We were poorer then, but a lot richer, too. They were the best days.
Now it's all glamour and motorhomes where we had just an old van.'*
Linda Dunlop

Throughout broad swathes of Northern Ireland, racing motorcycles are as integral a part of country life as cow-muck and barley. David Wallace's film *The Road Racers* begins with a herd of cows ambling along a leafy lane, before switching to Merv Robinson bump-starting a TZ Yamaha into ear-splitting life. To observers from almost anywhere else in the world – not to mention the sheep bolting in panic in an adjacent field – the juxtaposition of bucolic peace and screaming two-stroke engines jars wickedly. But to the farm folk of North Antrim, it's clearly just another day.

The film, an account of the 1977 season, was the first that many motorcycle fans had heard of a fast but cheerfully chaotic band of racers who went by the jaunty name of the Armoy Armada. The maritime connection owed everything to alliteration and nothing to the trio's roots, although it did presage Joey's capacity for shipwreck. The Armada had existed casually for some time in the friendship between Joey and Merv and Frank Kennedy, but was formalised, if that's the word, with the creation of an official Supporters Club in 1977. And the club was official mainly because Big Mel Murphy said so, and not least because the trio needed all the support they could get.

The Supporters Club met in the same Railway Tavern which would later become

At our house Joey wouldn't sit on a seat – scared of dirtying it I suppose

Joey with an early set of laurels in 1975, the year he really started to make his name. The helmet – a yellow Boeri – was a sloppy fit and had to be packed out with foam rubber. (Clifford McLean)

Jim Dunlop and Joey at the 1979 North-West 200, a day that began so well. (Clifford McLean)

Merv 'Robo' Robinson hustles a '354' Yamaha around Dundrod during the Ulster Grand Prix. (Clifford McLean)

auction which included, amongst other treasures, a loaf of bread. Overcome by the philanthropy of the occasion, the lucky winner donated his lot back to the auctioneer, who auctioned it again – slice by slice. As well as offering cash assistance to its principal riders, the club later sponsored a race at their local circuit for the 'Ace of Aghadowey', to the tune of over £200. This was a satisfactory arrangement all round, as Joey promptly won it.

Big Mel was responsible, aside from general enthusiasm and geeing people up, for the club's sole newsletter, published in 1978. Along with wife Marina – now a minicab driver in Ballymoney – Mel ran fund-raising dances at the Manor Hotel, quizzes and anything else to keep the boys in pistons and tyres. Sadly, Mel died of a heart attack in 1986 aged just 35. At the time Joey and Robert were 14 hours into a 24-hour bicycle ride in aid of Sports Aid. Joey donned a black bib to continue the ride in mourning. Having hoped to raise £300, the brothers found themselves with ten times that amount.

Mel put the same passion into club affairs

Joey's Bar and which his daughter Julie now runs. Funds came from membership fees of £2.00, plus £1.00 per month. Then there were the raffles and auctions. In 1978 in one event two motorcycles were offered as prizes, but the most memorable fund-raiser in the folk lore rapidly springing up around the Armada was an

and fund-raising as Joey and the boys gave to their racing. 'We drank in Joey's Bar – Lawrence Kelly had it then – from the year dot. We even had eating races to raise funds,' remembers Marina, still marvelling at the daftness of it all, 'boiled eggs, dry crackers, homemade hamburgers a foot across. Och it was some good craic. There'd be ten or 11 of us in the club. Everyone did their bit. We'd go to Mondello Park, take out the bikes and sleep in the van. But I can remember early on when Linda and Joey had nothing. There'd be just a packet of cornflakes in the house and nothing in the fridge. Joey never cared how he looked, and when he came in our house he'd never sit on a seat – scared of dirtying it, I suppose. He'd sit on his haunches for an hour or more. But it did bother him he couldn't give Linda more.

'Joey would go racing at the drop of a hat and whenever the call came, Mel would have to go too. He'd drop everything, leaving me with three kids, sometimes from Thursday to Tuesday if they went to England. Joey was a stubborn wee fella. If his mind was made up, that was it. But he was awful shy. He never talked much to me unless he'd had a few drinks, but he seemed glad to know you were around.' Stubborn or not, Marina named her youngest William Joseph, after Himself.

'Once,' adds Marina, 'Andy [Inglis] and Mel were delivering a load of Armada T-shirts and badges to Joey's. It was the day before the North-West so they were in a bit of a rush. Mel crashed the car, an old Skoda. Andy went flying up the road and just lay there – Mel thought he'd killed him at first. There were T-shirts and badges all over the road, the car was wrecked, and they burnt out the clutch of someone else's car towing it home – but they picked up every single T-shirt and every badge.'

Of the threesome, Frank Kennedy was the only one who actually hailed from Armoy, where he owned a garage with 'open-air show-room' – a field. Such as it was, the car business was inclined to take a back seat to the racing, not least because Saturday is the main day for selling used cars, but in Ireland Saturday is also race day. After a succession of four strokes – Hugh O'Kane's 7R, a 'Macchi and even a Manx

Norton – Frank moved to Yamaha twins in 1975, supported by the same Sam Taggart who would later help Joey out. In 1976 he led the North-West 200 by a distance until Sam's new Sparton triple gave up the ghost.

For a while in their early days, both Frank and Robo ran Ariel Arrows on the road. Andy Inglis recalls one of their customary scratches ending when first one plunged through a

Following Merv Robinson at the Ulster, 1975. Behind Joey is future Castrol Honda boss Neil Tuxworth. After making up for a poor start Joey crashed out, breaking a collarbone. (Clifford McLean)

Frank Kennedy, third member of the Armoy Armada, on his 500cc Sparton at the North West 200, 1976 (Clifford McLean)

Merv Robinson and Frank Kennedy (nearest camera) burning the midnight oil. (David Wallace)

Joey splashing through the puddles at the 1976 Tandragee 100 on John Rea's Yamsel. (Clifford McLean)

hedge, to be joined milliseconds later by the other crashing through precisely the same hole. On that occasion both got away lightly, but it wasn't always so. 'Frank was over six feet – big and clumsy,' remembers Willie. 'He was a helluva rider, better than they gave him credit for, but helluva big. When he fell off he'd go down heavy … he was always breaking stuff.'

That heaviness put him in intensive care at least once. *The Road Racers* film begins with Frank's attempts to ignore the pain of a smashed collarbone, and ends with two broken arms and a shattered thumb. 'I was just getting back to form when it sucked in a stone and seized on me,' as he ruefully explained to camera.

Other than crashing and poverty, the Armada's nemesis was the Dromara Destroyers, named after Ray McCullough's home town a dozen or so miles south of Belfast. The Destroyers – Ray himself, Brian Reid and Trevor Steele – were pre-eminent long before Merv and his gang of scruffy wannabes had the impertinence to become the Armada.

'I think the idea for the Destroyers came from Isaac Corbett and my mechanic Hubert Gibson,' chuckles McCullough today, 'but it was just a laugh – nothing really serious. We'd have do's to raise money, and they'd come to ours, and we'd go to theirs as well.' But to some of the fans, of course, there was much more to it than that.

As well as Joey, Merv and Frank, the Armada grew to include Jim, Joey's younger brother. Jim quickly became as adept as his elders at sliding off racing bikes. Eventually though, Joey became concerned at little brother's capacity for getting hurt whenever he fell off, and decided it was his fraternal duty to teach him 'how to crash properly'.

'Mind you,' remembered Linda, 'Joey was some boy to be learnin' him, because both of his collarbones were big and lumpy with being broken so much.' By then he'd broken them at least three times, at Maghaberry in '73, St Angelo in '74 and Dundrod in '75. Had Jim paused to think, he might have wondered if his big brother was the best possible tutor.

But Jim didn't pause to think and instead, a couple of days before the North-West 200, found himself sitting on the front wing of a car doing 40mph across Downhill Beach, near Castle Rock. Joey, sitting on the other wing, explained that the secret was in the landing, jumped off and rolled, unharmed, to a halt. 'Look, I'm OK. Now it's your turn.' The car turned round, picked Joey up and began another run. Jim, ever game, did as he was bid. His collarbone snapped and that was one Dunlop, at least, who'd miss the North-West.

Four years younger than his brother, Jim describes himself as 'a bit like Joey – our da always had engines lying around, and I could build one, down and up, when I was 15. Later there were always motorbikes around our house, and then this fella Jimmy Laverly, married to my sister Linda, left his Ariel Arrow at our place when it broke down. After school once me and another Jim – Joey's wife Linda's brother – fixed it and went down the road on it after school, and sort of got hooked. Joey also had an [Ariel] Arrow at the same time. There was a bit of a craze for 'em.'

One story gives a hint of Joey's capacity for astute observation before making his move – even after a few jars. 'I had an NSU Quickly, a 49cc moped,' remembers Jim. 'One night at about three in the morning, after a drink, we decided to see who could get it round the corner in front of our house flat-out. Merv went first, and fell off. Me next. I fell off too. Then Joey got on, and he wasn't so daft. He had the sense not to try it quite flat-out, stayed on, and won.'

Jim began racing – he's no idea of the year – when Joey lent him his old Suzuki Invader. By that time the cylinder barrels had been so trashed by enthusiastic tuning that Jim had to 'borrow the barrels off me da's road bike whenever I wanted to race. My first meeting was at Mondello Park. Of course Joey was much quicker, but later I was sometimes dicing with him, and he wasn't above giving you a wee shove. Merv, too. Once, at Kirkistown, he put me on the grass at the hairpin. "Och, racing's racing," he said after – so I knew to put him on the grass next time. That's how it went.'

After the Suzuki, Jim next got the hand-me-down air-cooled Yamaha, but it proved chronically unreliable. 'Then I rode Joey's old 350 Yamsel with the magnesium "Peter Williams" wheels, probably the bike he used for the 1976 TT. I'd gone to England, working to earn money to buy the bike, and got back to learn Martin Rea had bought it for me, which was brilliant. So Joey was sponsored by John Rea, me by Martin, and for a time another Rea brother, Noel, sponsored someone else. I remember me, Merv and Joey went to Oulton. I finished second, behind Ron Haslam and ahead of Joey.'

Joey's generosity in handing down bikes may have been genuine, but it was also conditional. 'When I started', recalls Jim, 'he made me switch to right-foot gearchange, like he used, in case he ever needed to ride the bike. Later he changed sides, so then I had to as well. But he was always a perfectionist. I used to throw the bike together before a race meeting, but he'd spend as long as it took to get it right.'

The Armoy Armada at the Bush Bridge, Armoy, during a walk to raise racing funds. Left to right: Jim Dunlop, Frank Kennedy, Joey, Merv Robinson. 'It wasn't serious,' said Joey's mum, 'just the bunch of them having fun.' (Clifford McLean)

Irish racing at its most spectacular: Joey chases Noel Hudson over the ferocious leaps of the Temple 100 road races in the late seventies. (Jim McBride)

Merv Robinson at the North-West in 1978. Note the 350 Yamaha's home-built laid-down rear shocks, as pioneered by Joey and his dad. (Clifford McLean)

Robert Dunlop came along too late to join the Armada. 'I wasn't that interested in racing at first – I was more into the girls,' he grins. 'But I had a road bike, a GT250 Suzuki. I fell off it *all* the time, once ran smack into the side of a car. It was breaking my mum's heart. Joey and them said I'd be far safer on the circuits than the road, lent me a 250 Yamsel – probably his 1976 TT bike. At the first meeting I couldn't get it started and ended up last, but I'd got the bug and that was that. A few local business people and friends clubbed together and bought me the bike. In fact I've still got it. I've never ridden a road bike since – far too dangerous.'

In his later years Joey would 'keep his hand in' working alongside both his brothers in Jim's steel erecting and roofing business, a trade not best known for obsessive perfectionism. But Joey was different. 'It used to send me crackers,' groans Jim, 'because time was money. But if a bloody great girder was just two millimetres

out, he'd have to get it right. And every single bolt would have to be just-so tight.'

Jim never did a TT, but competed in 'four or five' Manx Grands Prix and deserved to do better than a top placing of 'around fifth'. In 1979 he was leading the 350cc Newcomers race when the bike broke down at Schoolhouse Corner on the last lap. Joey, waiting for his brother in the pit, and with the shoe for once on the other foot, commented that he 'never realised it was so hard, waiting for someone to come round'.

The following year Jim rode Joey's TT-winning TZ750 to yet another breakdown. He stopped racing 'in around 1982 when I had no money and neither did Martin Rea. I tried to run the bikes myself but with no money spent on them, they kept breaking down. And I kept falling off. I thought if I stopped someone else might sponsor me, but no-one did. And that was that.' Afterwards he remained one of his brother's most loyal supporters,

If a girder was 2mm out he had to get it right

Joey on John Rea's TZ750 Yamaha at the Ulster in 1979, on his way to two wins in the meeting This same bike would win the Classic TT 10 months later.
(Clifford McLean)

With Shell's Keith Collow (left) and the Duke of Kent at the 1986 TT. (Joey Dunlop Family Collection)

Joey chats with Tony Rutter (left) and Stan Woods on the Ulster Grand Prix rostrum. (Clifford McLean – Pacemaker)

missing just one TT, 1986, between Joey's first win, and his last.

Jim's early retirement leaves him the bitter distinction of being the one Armada member still alive. In 1979 Frank Kennedy was killed in the same North-West 200 that claimed the life of the great Tom Herron. Precisely a year after that, wearing the same race number – 31 – Merv Robinson also died at the North-West.

As well as bringing Joey to the verge of packing racing in altogether, the loss of his hero Tom Herron and his closest racing buddies would gnaw at Joey's approach to the sport. It didn't happen overnight, but he would in future become a more clinical, less innocent rider than the happy-go-lucky, youthful Gurk. His superstitious aversion to the number 31 was the least significant of the legacies from that time. 'He once bought this old Cortina,' grins Andy Inglis, 'but I don't know why, because he wouldn't drive it as it had 31 in the number plate. I suggested he got it re-registered, which he did – and still wouldn't use it because the new numbers came to 31 if you added them up. So he sold it – to me.'

Helen, Merv's widow, is now happily re-married. Her husband, David Louden once loaned Joey a Mk1 GT Cortina which he crashed when the steering wheel came off in his hand. 'He'd tried hard to steer it,' chuckles David in Joey's defence. 'You could tell by the way all the threads on the steering column were ingrained in his fingers.'

Island Bound

'He liked riding there, right off, but wondered if he'd ever get to learn it.'
Curly Scott, mechanic, of Joey's TT début, 1976

Wal Handley began his first TT practice lap in the early 1920s by going the wrong way at the start. Joey began the greatest career in TT history better than that, but only just. Totally disorientated, he claimed to have stopped at Ballacraine crossroads, seven miles into his maiden lap. Here he waited for another rider to show him the way, successively tagging on to other riders as he lost the one before.

Joey was far from a novice on his first trip to the Isle of Man TT in 1976. Indeed, with seven seasons of Irish competition behind him, as well as outings at Knockhill, Oulton Park, Croft and elsewhere, he was something of a veteran, and certainly not fazed by street circuits. But never before had he attempted to race anywhere quite so daunting as this.

His crew that year were Willie, Curly Scott and Ernie Coates. Ernie had got to know Joey the previous year when Joey had unknowingly sabotaged sponsorship Ernie had been expecting from John Rea. It's typical of the affection Joey would generate throughout his career that the same man he'd accidentally compromised should become one of his most enthusiastic and enduring helpers.

Since no Manx-bound boats left from Ireland on the Sunday, the boys opted for the fishing boat crossing rather than miss the Cookstown 100 the previous Saturday. The one member of the crew who had never been to the

Previous page: *Joey pictured on the Yamsel at the North-West in 1977, the year of his first TT win.* (Gavan Caldwell – Pacemaker)

TT before was the man who really mattered. Willie had visited the races in September 1975, helping Merv Robinson's Manx Grand Prix début. He had come back a convert, as was Curly, who'd first been there 11 years before and had some idea of the task facing Joey: 'He liked riding there, right off, but wondered if he'd ever get to learn it and struggled to get the 100mph lap. He used to park me in the Inglewood [Hotel], do a few laps in the dark, and come back to the bar, learning it steady. He learned the road circuits at home the same way. Sometime he'd take me with him, explaining what he was doing as he drove along. Then he'd ask me for an assessment, and go out on his own for a few more laps. His driving was real smooth – just like on the bike.'

Wider recognition of what Curly already knew lay some years ahead, but that week it was a well-bred English public schoolboy who hogged the first headline. 'Masterly Mortimer' rang out the front page of *Motor Cycle News* on 9 June 1976. Nowhere was there the suggestion that a quiet-spoken Ballymoney man might have begun the first steps towards a TT fame

undreamed of by Chas Mortimer and all who had gone before. Back in 16th place, according to the programme, was one Joe Dunlop. Despite typically wet and misty Manx weather during practice, from a standing start he lapped at over 100mph. His fastest lap was his second, at 102.3mph. Averaging 99.83mph for the five-lap race, he gained a bronze replica and, along with Billy Guthrie and Courtney Junk, earned the club award for the Cookstown & District MCC. Tom Herron, the top Irish TT rider of the time, finished a lowly 26th, having pushed in from Hillberry when his Yamaha's chain jumped the sprockets.

In a busy week, Joey had further entries in the Lightweight (250cc), Senior, Production and Classic races. His fortunes were mixed. In the Senior, his 18th place on a '354' Yamsel brought another bronze replica in a race won by Herron but best remembered for John Williams' push-in on the final lap. In his other events Joey retired, although in one he had the odd distinction of doing so without ever sitting on the bike. The race was the 10-lap, two-rider Production TT in which he was paired with Billy Guthrie. Billy started, but retired their RD400 Yamaha with engine trouble after one lap, denying Joey a ride. This otherwise ignominious race carried another distinction, in that the duo began with the number which Joey would later make his own: '3'.

Whether by accident or design, in choosing to chase his car headlamps around the Mountain Circuit, Joey had hit right away on an approach which would last him for the rest of his career. Sammy Graham, later to join the Dunlop crew, remembers it well. 'He'd say you could see the bumps and ripples better at night in the car headlights. And sometimes he'd go a bit. Once there were six of us in a Cortina Estate, including Big Mel, and at the end of the lap Joey got out, bent down, and lit a cigarette off the brake disc.'

1976

The 1976 season had begun well enough, with a third place on the 350 at the North-West 200, but after the TT Joey was unstoppable, both at

Tom Herron, an inspiration to all Irish racers, was tragically killed at the North-West in 1979. (Clifford McLean – Pacemaker)

home and over the water. Wins piled up wherever he chose to unload his van: Mondello, Tandragee, Skerries, Fore, Aghadowey (which had replaced Maghaberry during 1975), Dundrod and Kirkistown. In the Southern 100 meeting, he recorded his first Isle of Man win in the Shell Invitation race, the first of 40 victories on the Billown Circuit. Another trip across the Irish Sea towards the end of the year brought wins at Croft and East Fortune.

The man Irish commentators were calling the Armoy Flier had sometimes had the beating of Ray McCullough, and was officially garlanded as the top Irish road racer of 1976. But it wasn't until the following year that Joey seemed truly to believe in himself as a legitimate Number One. If the breakthrough can be tied to any particular time, it came at Cookstown, one of his favourite road circuits. 'One of the best in Ireland,' he'd described it, 'but it's very, very narrow and very bumpy and hilly and there's not a straight-on.' Frank, less affectionately, elaborated on the lack of 'straight-ons' – what we'd now call run-offs – with the observation that 'there's always something to hit ... concrete posts and stone walls, right around the whole place.'

When the 500 race began, Joey already had two second places – and would have done better had a clutch cable not snapped. He and that man McCullough were dicing for the lead again. Previously, Joey admitted, he had ridden in awe of McCullough. 'I'd get ahead, and get frightened ... feel like I must be going too fast.' But this time it was different. Something clicked, something fell into place and he won, with a record lap at 101.25mph.

Ten years Joey's senior, McCullough would surely have been far better known overseas had he not spurned the TT, which he considered 'too much trouble ... too expensive ... and too many early mornings.' In a career beginning in 1960 (inevitably, on a Triumph Tiger Cub) and ending in 1984, he won practically everything worth winning in Ireland. McCullough first began to take a serious interest in Joey in 1975 when both campaigned 350 Yamahas for the first time. Amongst many furious dices, the ones that stand out are a head-to-head at

Joey on the 350 Yamsel at the North-West 200, 1977. Second on his 250 to Tony Rutter was his best North-West result so far. (Clifford McLean)

Temple when Joey overshot the last corner, and this day at Cookstown.

As men, the two were poles apart. McCullough was a thoughtful, well-educated technician at Belfast's Queens University, whilst Joey was a diesel fitter-cum-lorry driver from the sticks. But the respect each had for the other was palpable. 'Quick but safe' is how Ray described even the young Joey. 'He was never riding the hedges and ditches like some. He was good to race against ... very quiet, but every now and then he'd come over and we'd have a long conversation about the bikes, about the racing. He was a smart mechanic, good at setting up the bikes. It was Joey who worked out why we were getting beat on the Yamsels at the short circuits. He reckoned the long swing arm made the bike step out at slow corners, so shortened his. And it worked, so I shortened mine too.'

From Cookstown, Joey and the boys went on the now traditional fishing boat to the Isle of Man. His crew included Willie, as ever,

Joey at Aghadowey in 1977, riding the same Seeley-framed TZ750 on which he would win his first Isle of Man TT. Note the 'Herron replica' crossover exhaust. (Jim McBride)

Something about Joey made folk want to join in the adventure

younger brother Jim, Curly Scott, Jackie Graham, Andy Inglis and Big Mel Murphy. Andy was known as 'the storeman' because he knew Joey's garage better than Joey did. If anyone needed to find anything, it was him they would ask.

In the early days the whole crew would stay with former Irish racer Norman Dunne at Number 1, Hutchinson Square. The Walpole, as it was only occasionally known, was the first of a succession of 'Irish Embassies' infamous for the sheer volume of booze that went in and never came out. In later years Honda would offer to accommodate Joey somewhere more lavish, but he always stayed with his gang, where he could – and often did – behave more or less as he pleased. At the time, of course, with his only personal sponsor being the Ballymoney dole office, he had little choice but to make the most of ever-willing friends.

Nor was he a model of modern labour relations, as Jackie Graham remembers: 'You never knew you were going until the last bloody minute. One year we were on our way to Cookstown and he asked if I was going to the TT – and he was going there straight from Cookstown. I hadn't even packed. He was inconsiderate, but he was kind too. If sponsors

weren't paying our wages, he'd always offer – but me and Sammy would rather work for nothing than take Joey's money.' Sammy, Jackie's son, who joined the team as a mechanic two years later, recalls the talent Joey had for making people feel privileged to be part of it all. No-one even so much as hinted that there might be anything mercenary in his motives. Something about Joey, about his special combination of shyness and determination, reached out and made hard men drop everything to join in the adventure. It would be the same when he became a factory rider. In the meantime, laughs Sammy, 'He'd ring up and say "are you busy?". Even if you were, for Joey you'd say you weren't. Sometimes he'd ask you to help him for TT fortnight on the day he was leaving. Before that, you wouldn't have a clue.'

In TT week, Linda was more peripheral still. 'I was very nervous then – I didn't go to the grandstand. I stayed at Norman Dunne's instead with Julie and the radio, listening to the races when he won in 1977. In 1980 I was seven months pregnant with Donna, so I listened to that win on the radio too. The first time I went to the grandstand was when he won his 14th TT. I'd got it into my head that if I went there, he wouldn't win, which he thought was silly.'

1977

In 1977 there was nothing silly about Joey's riding in what was still only his second TT, although it was Phil Read who grabbed the headlines with wins in both the Formula One and Senior races. (One week later the headlines read 'Read Faces Court' after he crashed an uninsured, slick-shod race bike on public roads.) Joey's press ran to a modest front page bullet noting that 'Irishman Joe Dunlop won Friday's Jubilee TT and became the third fastest man round the Mountain Course.' Inside, under the heading 'Joey's Jubilee', journalist Norrie White described how 'the admiral of the Armoy Armada' had won by 51.6 seconds from George Fogarty of Blackburn – father of Carl.

The race was the Schweppes Jubilee Classic,

an invitation event commemorating 70 years of TT racing. Special rules meant that slick tyres were not allowed and, in truth, the very top names were also absent. Riding John Rea's TZ750, Joey had topped the practice rankings for the class with 106.80mph, helped in part by tuition from Tom Herron. 'Before he dashed off to the Yugoslav GP,' explained Joey, 'Tom had shown me the way round and I learned an awful lot. There were bends I was struggling with but when he explained the lines I was even able to take them flat-out on my 750.'

The Yamaha in question was a curious mix of four cylinder engine from the bike bought for Daytona, and George McQuilty's three-year-old Seeley twin-shock chassis intended for a Suzuki. 'The exhausts were the big problem,' explained Willie, who 'sort of copied' the crossover pipe layout from Herron's latest TZ. After 'measuring' its elaborate curves with nothing more precise than his penknife, Willie

somehow got the dimensions close enough to make it work.

Despite his practice performance, Joey's first TT win was far from trouble-free. In fact, it would be Braddan Bridge before the bike would run on all four cylinders. Ominously for every other TT pretender, his fastest lap was his first, just 20 seconds slower than Mick Grant's new outright record. In future years he'd use similarly blistering early pace to demoralise the opposition.

But meanwhile, there were still three more laps to negotiate, beset by problems with the exhaust, and concern over the rear tyre. During practice the bike's relatively harsh twin-shock suspension had been wrecking the treaded Dunlop rear tyres in as few as two laps, yet now they had to handle twice that distance at full race speed. When a security wire retaining one of the exhausts came loose, Jim Dunlop was 'terrified they'd black flag him, or if they didn't,

Joey at Quarter Bridge in 1978, his first Formula One TT, and his first Honda ride, on Dave Mason's 812 Devimead. (Nick Nicholls)

Racing Hector Neill's RG500 Suzuki at Aghadowey, probably in the spring of 1979. On Joey's back wheel is – who else? – Merv Robinson. (Jim McBride)

Opposite: Joey getting plenty of air at Temple in 1979. Irish road racing is as much low-level flying as motorcycling. (Clifford McLean)

because the other guy in the pit had disappeared for a smoke, so if he'd pitted I'd have been there on my own.' In the event Joey pitted only for one routine fuel stop, and had sufficient spare time to pull over at Ramsey and check the rear tyre.

Ernie Coates remembers it well. 'I was up on the mountain. When I heard he was leading I ran back to the Bungalow like a mad thing and started signalling. I didn't have a board or anything – I suppose I just waved my arms about.' Having thus proved his mettle, Ernie would spend much of the next decade high on Snaefell with a blackboard, until Joey decided

he'd be better employed in his pit.

From the rostrum Joey admitted that prior to the TT his biggest-ever racing prize had been £100 plus 50 gallons of free petrol. So he was 'a bit staggered' with the £1000 of Schweppes money, although less so that the jobsworth at the Schweppes hospitality tent wouldn't let him in, until Norrie White pointed out what a great story that would make. Earlier in the week he'd won a further £700 with tenth place in the Lightweight, seventh in the Classic and an impressive fourth in a weather-shortened Senior, riding the 350 twin. He later reckoned that an unscheduled stop to have his chain adjusted in the Classic cost him third place and another £325. Still, with £1700 in the kitty, maybe Linda could have a washing machine, after all. On the way home, not surprisingly, Joey was already 'fair buzzing' about the prospects for the following year's TT.

1978

In fact the 1978 TT would be a sentimental triumph for Mike Hailwood, a major disappointment for Joey, and a tragedy for the races themselves. After becoming the first man to break the 20-minute barrier in practice (19:54.0/113.75mph), America's Pat Hennen crashed out of Monday's Senior race, sustaining permanent brain damage. On the same day, popular sidecar aces Mac Hobson and Kenny Birch died on Bray Hill.

Perhaps the pattern had been set at Daytona, where the 200-miler was then one of the most important events on the road-racing calendar. Competing at the Florida raceway the previous year had represented a major leap in class for Joey and the boys. In order to tame the speeds of the 750cc two-strokes around the Speedway banking, the authorities had decreed the fitting of intake restrictors. Getting the bikes to carburate was causing mayhem for even the most technically sophisticated crews – a category which probably did not include Joey's gang. As Willie remarked many years later, 'In those days we knew nothing about squish bands or compression volumes and stuff like that. We just bolted 'em together.' Thus bolted, Joey's 750 bogged down at the start of the main event. After he had ridden like a dervish to get into the top 20, the engine finally blew. His eighth place on Sam Taggart's bike in a high-class 250cc race won by Hansford from Mamola was a fine showing but thin consolation.

'I organised our freight that year,' admits Ernie Coates. 'Mike Trimby organised everything for the English boys, but we thought they'd think they were above us, so we did it ourselves. Sometimes we thought we were being treated like poor relations. Maybe it was only in our heads, but Joey was scruffy where they were tidy. He cared more about the bike

It's 1979, and Joey hustles the TZ750 on the day of his first North-West 200 win – and the day Tom Herron and Frank Kennedy died. (Clifford McLean)

Opposite: Towing an atmospheric cloud of two-stroke exhaust, racing's most famous Number 3 leads the field at his local North-West 200 circuit. (Clifford McLean – Pacemaker)

going right than working on himself.'

Later Joy and Ernie Coates journeyed to Holland to collect an ex Jon Ekerold Mercedes van for John Rea. 'John asked me to go along because Joey couldn't speak to anyone, let alone ask directions. And he couldn't really read, let alone read a map.' From there they headed for Denmark to pick up some motocross bikes and along the way somehow found themselves buying a TZ750 on John Rea's behalf, although they didn't get around to telling John until later. 'Yamaha had just finished making them,' Ernie explains, 'so good ones were rare.' Ernie suspects this was the machine on which Joey would take his first major TT win, the 1980 Classic. In the meantime there were more unproductive overseas events, first at Brands Hatch and later at Paul Ricard for the Formula 750 series.

Ernie describes a French trip more remarkable for Joey's off-track resourcefulness than his riding, which yielded a mid-field place, way behind Cecotto and Roberts. 'On the way home there were big snows in France and we ground to a halt on this hill, solid with trucks all stuck in a line against the hedge. I woke Joey

up. He took a few seconds to take it all in, then took the chains off the bikes, and all our spare chains, and wrapped 'em round the wheels – snow chains. We were the only ones who made the boat that night.'

Joey was glad to get back to Ireland. Wins at Cookstown and Dundrod appeared to put him in the mood for the Isle of Man, but it was not to be. His best result of the week was fifth in the lesser known Formula Two event, and only then after he inherited a somewhat improbable ride on a Benelli 550 from Snuffy Davies, 'just to get in some more laps'. The Classic, Senior and Formula One races all brought retirement, leavened only by a lowly eleventh in the Lightweight TT – albeit one place ahead of Mike Hailwood.

1979

If 1979 delivered a succession of first class results, it was also a year which brought home the potential for pain and loss that lies behind all road racing. It began innocuously enough, with yet another troubled performance at Daytona when the 750 ran a crank and the 250 could manage no better than twelfth place. After a fruitless trip to Paul Ricard, he lost out to future team-mate Ron Haslam at Oulton Park, before getting back to the proper business of Irish roads.

It was Saturday 26 May. The North-West 200, that seaside triangle just 10 miles down the road from Ballymoney, had never been Joey's favourite. Yet cruelly, his first win there coincided with the most tragic day of his career. In winning the Anglo-Irish Match Race from Mick Grant, Joey helped Tom Herron's squad to a resounding 193–119 point victory over Tony Rutter's Englishmen. With a fastest lap at an astonishing 124.66mph, he was in unstoppable form, and went on to beat Reg Marshall by inches in the 1000cc feature race.

It was only after the finish of his greatest Irish win so far that he learned of the terrible events behind. Tom Herron was dead. The hard-riding and hard-partying man of Mourne, every Irish rider's inspiration, and twice Joey's course tutor on the Isle of Man, died when he

crashed at Juniper Hill on the last lap of Joey's finest race. It was unthinkable, but there was worse. Frank Kennedy, too, was fatally injured after colliding with Kevin Stowe in the same tainted event. Stowe, Roy Jeffreys and Mick Grant were badly hurt and Scotland's Brian Hamilton died after crashing in the 350cc race. Ulster was numbed.

Days later, Joey was on the Isle of Man. If we can be sure of anything, it's that he was not 'fair buzzing' this time around. Palpably de-tuned by recent events, it was maybe not ideal that his opening race would find him mounted on his least competitive Formula One machine – a Benelli 900 Sei loaned by UK importers, Agrati Sales. It was slow, unwieldy and uncom-petitive, and he was surely delighted to park it on lap two. Both the Senior and Lightweight

events brought further retirements, the latter when he ran out of fuel. A 13th in the Formula Two TT on another Benelli, with not even a bronze replica, was little better.

Everyone who was there that year (and many who weren't) recalls that the highlight of race week was the stirring duel between Alex George and Mike Hailwood in the £30,000 Schweppes Classic. Joey's role in 'the richest race in the world' was more modest, but sixth was a solid, if unspectacular, result. His best lap, narrowly below 110mph, was again a personal best.

The TT spark may have stuttered, but a return to Ireland brought a rash of wins on road and short circuits alike. Back on The Island for July's Southern 100, he took no less than four wins, a feat he wouldn't equal for 12

Joey winning the 500cc Ulster Grand Prix in 1979. He enjoyed far better fortune with the square four Suzuki than with the 500cc Yamaha four. (Clifford McLean)

years. Then came Ireland's blue riband event, the Ulster Grand Prix, and maiden victories for Joey in both the 500cc and Superbike races ahead of John Newbold and Roger Marshall. In between times, he and the boys embarked on one of their most ambitious overseas epics yet, hauling their customary stock of beans, steak and vodka to the French Grand Prix at Le Mans, then to races in Holland, Germany, Austria and Yugoslavia.

1980

The new decade began with a repeat of old disappointments. At Daytona, despite a misfire, Joey lay in the top ten when it began to rain and the race was stopped. In the re-start the misfire worsened as the Yamaha's ignition

gave up. But the North-West 200 was far worse. Joey finished only the 350cc race, in fourth, behind Williams, Rutter and Tonkin. Riding a four cylinder TZ in the 500cc race he started badly, but swooped past Grant, Newbold and Avant into the lead, only for the Yamaha's gearbox to seize after setting fastest lap of the meeting at 121.97mph.

'The gears were too hard,' insists Jackie Graham of the TZ500, 'they just shattered like glass. Joey didn't trust the bike after that.' Indeed he didn't, but that wasn't the main issue. The meeting had claimed the life of Merv Robinson, his closest ally in racing. The loss would bring Joey to the verge of retirement. 'It was Merv who started me racing,' he told Norrie White. 'My wife wants me to pack up but I couldn't miss the TT. I wasn't going to do

Joey leads the pack at Dundrod in 1979, on his way to a superb Ulster GP double.
(Clifford McLean – Pacemaker)

Cookstown but decided that I'd better race to get my confidence back before the TT.'

Yet even that small ambition proved cruelly fated, for at Cookstown several of Joey's friends were hurt when their bikes caught fire after crashing. 'I can't see much future for racing on public roads after all the accidents this year,' admitted a desolated Joey. 'I'm hoping to get a 500 Suzuki for UK meetings after the TT. If I get a Suzuki, I may concentrate on short circuit racing.'

In the meantime, with the TZ500 so troublesome, Joey tackled the TT with the usual array of 250, 350, 354 and 750cc Yamahas. It was now three years since his last success, and although he was clearly a solid TT performer, few non-Irish observers recognised the force he would become. Indeed the big story in *Motor Cycle News* on the eve of the TT was of Barry Sheene damaging his left pinkie at the French GP.

With one glorious exception it wasn't a vintage Dunlop TT. Ninth in the Talbot Senior and 12th in the Lightweight were nothing to write home about. But a week after lamenting Bazza's misfortune, the *Motor Cycle News* front page screamed of 'Joe's Irish Jig – at 115mph'. Race reports lauded 'the quiet Ulsterman' who had become the fastest man in TT history in winning the Classic TT: 'Mick Grant rode the hardest TT race of his career on his works 998cc Honda but could not match Joey Dunlop on his 750 Yamaha.'

Yet in practice Joey had managed no better than sixth on the Rea TZ750, with a best lap at 108.54mph. It wasn't until the night before the race that the team got its hands on a spare crankshaft. Joey had worked on the bike until 2.30am, leaving Jackie and Willie to continue race preparations. 'Throughout practice I just couldn't get the big Yamaha to handle,' he later admitted. 'Then at the last minute we noticed the rear wheel spacers were in back-to-front.

'The motor was OK – the same one I rode on The Island two years ago. I had an eight gallon tank made so I'd only have to stop once for juice – we got an extra three inches welded in at a place in Ballasalla at 1 o'clock on the night before the race.'

Apart from being, according to Jackie, 'the

ugliest thing you've ever seen,' the tank was very big and very heavy. 'It was a bit of a monster for a little guy like me,' Joey explained after the race, 'especially as I couldn't find a screen tall enough to cover the tank and my helmet. At Ballacraine on the first lap, two of the tank straps broke. I was really scared at [the big jump at] Ballaugh that the tank would come off the frame and pull the fuel pipes off.'

It's difficult now to appreciate the enormity of what Joey and his crew had achieved. If the 1977 win was in something of a second division TT, this was the real thing. And it was a triumph for a bunch of Irish country boys over the might of the factory Hondas. Even though Joey didn't rush during his one fuel stop – 'I wasn't taking any chances after running out in last year's 250 race' – with two stops to make, even Honda's high-tech quickfill system, worth over half a minute, could not turn it around for Grant. At Ballacraine on the last lap, the lead was just 0.3 seconds, but Joey's record lap put the result beyond doubt. Grant, struggling to use top gear on his 1062cc works engine, was 20.4 seconds in arrears at the finish.

'I was being egged on by loads of Irish fans all around the circuit,' grinned Joey after the race. 'I knew the lap record was in danger on the last lap. With the petrol weight gone, the bike was going as smooth as a Bushmills. My only problem was that the last rip-off [visor] wouldn't come off at any price, and with the number of flies which committed suicide on it, it was difficult seeing out.'

For the rest of his career Joey would nominate this as his most satisfying TT victory. Part of its appeal was the fact of 'beating all the factory riders by fooling them.' But of equal importance was being able to dedicate his triumph to the memory of his greatest racing friend. Merv, as much as Joey, won the Classic TT that year. 'I'd told everyone that this was going to be the last one,' he explained after announcing that he'd be celebrating in Ireland, 'but obviously I'll have to think again about that. When Merv was killed I cancelled all my entries apart from the TT, but now I might do a few English meetings as well. I might even spend a bob or two out of the £8000 I've won.'

I can't see much future for racing on public roads after all the accidents this year

Opposite: *Joey's first factory ride came from Heron Suzuki in 1980, when he handed Graeme Crosby the world F1 title on a platter.* (Clifford McLean)

Chapter Six

Factory Joey

'He was the ultimate privateer – he'd never let on to anyone what he was doing, how the bike was working, anything like that. He'd help anyone – except with settings, where he believed he should never give anything away, including to our own engineers. This made life fairly interesting!'

Barry Symmons, Honda Britain race boss

After the 1980 TT, Mick Grant stood precariously at the top of the world Formula One rankings with 15 points, three more than Heron Suzuki's Graeme Crosby. With the championship comprising just two rounds that year – the Isle of Man and Ulster Grand Prix – everything hinged on Dundrod. Suzuki, seeking an extra margin for their man, turned their collective gaze to Ballymoney. And so it was that, at the beginning of August 1980, William Joseph became an official factory rider with the aim of helping a Kiwi to the world crown. As it turned out, with Joey's help, Croz also came within a whisker of taking the British F1 title as well.

'I already knew Joey through Hector Neill at the Isle of Man,' explained Suzuki team boss, Rex White. 'He was obviously a star on the Irish circuits, so when we were pushing for the title I suggested we took him on. He rode at Silverstone and a couple of other places as well as Dundrod, and I think he surprised a few people on the short circuits.'

Did he not! Sunday, 10 August was Joey's maiden competitive ride for Suzuki, in round seven of the ten-round British championship. He was fortunate in that, of all the English short circuits, his début was at the one most likely to suit him – the fast sweeping curves of

Easter 1981, and the new Honda teamster is out of his depth taking on the USA at Brands Hatch in the annual match races. (Nick Nicholls)

The 'job' was a high-speed battle of cat and mouse

Silverstone. In practice he was 'just told not to fall off,' recalls Jackie Graham, 'so he was cruising around, taking it easy. But he wasn't actually far off the pace, so I told him he should go for it a bit. Next thing, Joey's on pole – and Crosby, who thought he'd got pole stitched up, had to put his gear back on and go out all over again.'

In the race, Joey took an early lead, with Crosby some distance behind. On a strange bike, on an unfamiliar circuit, he controlled the race like a veteran, repeatedly overtaking and holding up John Newbold while his new team-mate made up ground. At the finish, he placed a dutiful second to hand Croz the win and 15 championship points.

If Joey could kick ass like that in Northamptonshire, what could he do at Dundrod six days later? The answer was possibly the most one-sided, complicated and comical World Championship round ever run. Joey may have felt under pressure but it certainly didn't show. He was in scintillating form. Having warmed up by winning the 250 race from Donnie Robinson and the evergreen Ray McCullough, Joey took the McNaughton Blair Classic race from Roger Marshall's TZ750 with a record lap at 118.95mph. Then, to the utter delight of his countrymen, Joey showed he was The Man at World Championship level too.

Essentially Joey's job was to ride Suzuki shotgun for Croz, whilst Ron Haslam did the same for Mick Grant's Honda. Rex White remembers it well: 'He knew exactly what he had to do – help Croz stay in front and Granty behind – and he did it perfectly. It must have been the first time he'd ever been asked to lose a race, but he understood, and did a great job.'

The 'job' was a desperate battle of high-speed cat and mouse as Dunlop, easily the fastest man in the field, strove to give his team-mate the edge. That may sound simple, but in the to-and-fro of the 39-minute race, and with relatively primitive public address and time-keeping systems, it was not. Sammy Graham, giving signals at the hairpin, remembers it as being 'pretty confusing'. The title was eventually sealed for Crosby when Joey handed him the win, with Grant third and Haslam fourth after sliding off trying to let his team-mate through at the hairpin. 'I owe everything to my Suzuki team-mate Joey Dunlop', was the least Crosby could have said. A day later Joey got an even better present when Linda gave birth to their second daughter, Donna, at hospital in Ballymoney.

After Dundrod, Joey returned to the domes-tic Formula One series, with yet another second place behind Crosby at Donington Park. However, he struggled in the final two rounds – ninth at Cadwell after a 'massive' high-side in practice, and fifth at Brands Hatch's October Powerbike meeting. Aided by team orders, Grant narrowly won the title for Honda.

During Joey's run in the Heron Suzuki squad, Crosby had closed from 41 points in arrears to a mere three at the finish. It was clear that team boss Rex White, at least, wanted his services for the following year: 'I think from now on you'll be seeing much better form from him at short circuits … with Joey in the Formula One team next season, we could work wonders.'

Sadly for Suzuki, it wasn't to be, although

In 1982 Joey signed his first personal sponsorship deal, with Top Tek Helmets. (Don Morley)

As well as having the red T-shirt and pulling on the gloves in correct order, Joey's superstitions included not donning race boots too soon. (Don Morley)

Opposite: *Joey (left), Ron Haslam and Wayne Gardner contemplating the big Honda four in 1982.* (Joey Dunlop Family Collection)

1981

The instrument by which Joey switched to the rival Honda camp was the same Davy Wood with whom Joey had scrapped on his Tiger Cub way back in the Sixties at Maghaberry. In 1980 Davy was reigning Irish 200cc champion, but more pertinently worked in tobacco marketing and understood something of the commercial side of sport. This was a subject which would remain a profound and uninteresting mystery to Joey.

Davy and Joey 'weren't drinking buddies, we just knew each other in the paddock. I remember in '74 at the Tandragee 100, we were both riding 250 Yams, but mine blew to bits. I was due at Mondello for the Leinster the next day, so Joey just loaned me his 250. That was the sort of fella he was.'

Now Davy, as befits a man who occupies a house named 'Hondarosa', is something of a Honda fan. 'I was riding 182cc Honda twins,' he explains, 'so I was in with Honda. John Rea and I thought they might be worth a call, so I rang Gerald Davidson. He was interested, told us to put Joey on a plane. So me, John and Joey – him with a suit and a haircut – are collected from the airport in a Rolls-Royce and taken to Chiswick to meet Gerald and Barry Symmons. According to John, we got him about six times what the Suzuki deal would have been worth.'

Joining Honda put Joey under the wing of race boss Barry Symmons – a stern, headmasterish character with a reputation for being as controlled and precise as Joey was easy-going and casual. On the face of it this was a relationship made anywhere but heaven. For his part Symmons had 'first really noticed Joey at the TT in 1980. We had our own super-quick fillers and I remember looking at this really decrepit-looking bike in the next pit to ours, using slow fillers, and thinking this really wasn't fair – and it was Joey and he won the race! In a way I was rather pleased that justice had been done.

'So when we needed someone to head up our TT programme, he was the obvious choice. He was very suspicious of contracts – and of people wearing ties, so I soon learned not to

there were negotiations. 'He turned up for the meeting with Peter Agg and Maurice Knight in an articulated lorry,' recalls White with a chuckle. 'He'd been on the Continent and just dropped by at [Suzuki's HQ on] Bedington Lane on the way home, and parked it outside. We offered him a contract for 1981, but he didn't come back to us, didn't haggle, and the next thing we knew he'd signed for Honda.'

wear one. In his first contract he kept insisting on a clause about 'none of them women', which at first we couldn't understand. It turned out he didn't want to appear with publicity girls at shows. He thought Linda wouldn't like it.'

There was also a language problem to overcome. Now Ballymoney folk are fond of telling you 'Och we're just broad, with a wee bit of Scots in us. You should hear them in Ballymena – they really speak slang'. Ballymena is 12 miles down the Belfast road, Chiswick a few hundred miles beyond that, and Honda Japan several thousand, but Chiswick was light years nearer to Tokyo than Joey-speak.

The first factory bikes were pig-ugly RCB straight fours, developed by RSC – Racing Service Centre, the forerunner of HRC. When

Joey heads team-mate Ron Haslam at Dundrod, 21 August 1982. Ron won, but second was enough to give Joey his first world title. (Bill McLeod)

Joey tested the factory Formula One bike for the first time at Jurby Airfield in 1981, he offered some technical analysis to his new employers: 'It's dinlin' a w'een'. Embarrassed silence. The Japanese technicians were baffled. But surely they could comprehend good Ballymoney argot for 'the forks are not working as they should'?

'The Japanese couldn't understand a word Joey said,' explains Symmons. 'We had to translate. But we had an awful job understanding him at first, until we twigged that it helped if we slowed him down. Then he'd go home for the winter, and you'd have to start all over again the next season. In the end I worked out his code for how the bike was going. 'Dead-on' meant everything was perfect. 'It's not too bad' meant it was pretty dire, but 'It'll do' meant it was good enough to race and win.'

Communication problems may have been novel to Joey's Honda bosses, but to Joey they were old hat. Davy Wood still chuckles at the memory of Joey trying to make himself understood, in a race paddock crackling with noisy two-stroke engines, through a crash helmet, to Jackie Graham who, even then, was half deaf. 'How they worked anything out,' he grins, 'I'll never know.'

'Later he made a massive effort to make himself understood,' reckons Honda mechanic Nick Goodison. 'We'd talk about it a lot. He knew it was important. But often you'd look at his body language and try to guess. And sometimes you'd see him leap off the bike and grab the spanners himself, because that was easier.'

Even many years later, Joey-speak could give trouble. Another mechanic, Slick Bass, still giggles when he recalls practice at the British Grand Prix meeting in 1987. 'Joey came flying into the pit and said something … rat-a-tat … but we didn't have a clue what, partly because we couldn't see his lips move inside his helmet. So I put the stand under the bike. No, that wasn't it. Someone suggested he wanted a bump-start. No, he didn't like that either. It turned out he'd just dropped into the pits for a breather.'

Even Davy Wood sometimes struggled, as when he responded the first time Joey complained of being 'starving'. Ten minutes later Davy returned with an armful of fish and chips, only to discover that in Ballymoney 'starving' means 'cold'. But sometimes, the effect was contrived. That same Ballymoney accent could be a useful foil against outsiders – especially anyone English or Japanese – to stop them finding out things he would rather they didn't know.

Joey's loyalty to Honda, to Arai and to other sponsors became legendary, but although he'd sometimes go to extraordinary lengths to help the squad, he was never a natural team player. Symmons's description of him as the 'ultimate privateer' is revealing. 'Many leading English riders seemed to think that Joey was just a flash in the pan, that he couldn't possibly sustain it. And with his long hair and scruffy looks, they couldn't understand how on earth Honda could use him to promote their products. But he knew that being with a team was different. He asked what I thought he could do to fit into the team. He was keen to help us – but we understood that he was very much a motorcyclist's motorcyclist. For instance we soon learned to deter the media from making appointments with him. Arranging, say, to meet him in two hours just meant that he'd spend two hours worrying about what he was going to do, and that he probably wouldn't turn up anyway.

'It was with the bikes that he was best. He was actually a good engineer. He was the first man to build an aluminium chassis for a Formula One bike – although he'd sometimes forget something obvious, like bolting up the swing-arm.

'Without Linda he was his own worst enemy – helpless in lots of ways. Most of the time he was all right because everything stayed in his van, so he never needed to pack. But if he did, he was in trouble. He once turned up at Suzuka and I saw that he was limping. It turned out that he'd brought two left race boots. I took him down to Kushitani for some new ones, where they fell in love with him. The next year he turned up for the Eight-hours with two left boots.'

It's tempting to look back and imagine that Joey and Honda hit it off right away. But that

was certainly not the case. True, he brought them the Formula One world crown in his second season, but it was by far the least convincing of all his titles. And it would be 1983 and Joey's third year with Honda before he brought them a first TT win.

Joey insisted that his first Honda contract should have a clause about 'none of them women'. As he got older he became a little more laid-back, as with this Miss North-West 200. (Clifford McLean – Pacemaker)

'Rent-a-Merc.' It could almost have been Joey's catchphrase. (Stephen Davison – Pacemaker)

Opposite: *Tipping the big Honda into Keppel Gate on route to finishing second to team-mate Ron Haslam in the 1982 F1 TT.* (Don Morley)

event. Troubled more by an errant dog under Portrush railway bridge than by the rest of the field, he was so far ahead of Steve Parrish and Dennis Ireland on the final lap that he stopped to ask his ex-sponsor, Johnny Rea, whether he wanted a lift back to the paddock. Riding a 1123cc Honda, his fastest lap was a startling 121.06mph, on the revised Portrush circuit.

As a shake-down to the TT, it looked perfect. But The Island was to provide one of the most unsavoury weeks of Joey's long career. In the opening Formula One race, reigning champion Crosby was unable to start on time and, with his clock evidently ticking, was moved to the back of the grid.

Joey led early on but was slowed by a slight misfire after a bird-strike, then lost time changing a shredded rear tyre. 'With either the tyre problem or the misfire I could have won,' he declared later, 'but not with both.' This was disappointing for Joey, true. But so far as Honda was concerned, it allowed Ron Haslam to win and retain their one-two. Then Suzuki's Martyn Ogborne put in a protest. As a result, Graeme Crosby was credited with the time lost on the grid and installed as the winner 2½ hours after the race had finished.

The Honda camp, with some justification, was livid. Rumours of protest flew around The Island, but none quite captured the bizarre reality that lined up for Friday's Classic TT. No longer were Honda Britain clad in patriotic red, white and blue. Not only the bikes, but the riders' kit was as black as Honda's corporate mood. Manx Leathers, who had run up new suits for Joey, Haslam and Alex George, were reported to be in a state of shock.

Whatever Honda's pleas to the contrary, their riders looked bemused and embarrassed by the whole affair. But if it affected Joey's riding, this didn't show. From trailing Crosby by five seconds after lap one, Joey took 1.8 seconds off his own record next time around. By the Bungalow commentary station on lap three, he had edged into a narrow lead at an even more furious pace. But the extra speed exacted a cruel price – he ran out of fuel on the climb from Hillberry. 'The petrol ran out at Cronk-ny-Mona,' he explained afterwards, 'and

Yet Joey's first season with the Honda squad began auspiciously – for Joey if not for Honda – when, on 14 April the Manx mint introduced a 'double crown' TT coin, depicting him winning the previous year's Classic TT, on a Yamaha. One month later, just a few miles from home in the North-West 200, with his main rivals retiring he cake-walked the main

Pausing self-consciously for a photograph before setting out to film his awesome lap of the TT course at the 1983 Manx Grand Prix. (Honda Europe)

I freewheeled to the Nook, then began the push. The bike is so big … I only made it to the pits by taking it one telegraph pole at a time, then having a little rest.'

Refuelled and pumped up with adrenaline, Joey set off to recapture lost time. From Ballacraine to Ballacraine he recorded an unofficial lap time of 19:22 – around 117mph and way inside the record. But the chase was too much. Leaving the Gooseneck on lap five he 'must have taken her to 9000rpm once too often' and the cam chain broke.

The result was that the black protest, far from convincing observers of Honda's case, had simply drawn more attention to a cock-up in their race strategy. To compound the team's misery, Haslam went out with ignition troubles when lying third, leaving Crosby and Grant to display-ride to an easy Suzuki one-two. Only Alex George, third at the finish, was left to fly Honda's black flag. Symmons blamed the miscalculation on the race's furious pace: 'We reckoned on 9.2 litres per lap. But we didn't reckon on three 115mph laps.'

Honda's Gerald Davidson used the pages of *Motor Cycle News* to explain what even ACU chairman Vernon Cooper described as 'a product of a tiny mind'. He said: 'Our action was intended as a dignified and serious demonstration. Our riders were not in the least reluctant to support this. My last word on the TT we wish to forget is an apology to Joey Dunlop's many supporters. It was heart-breaking for him to run out of fuel having broken the lap record. All I can say is that we used our largest tank and it was full … even our most pessimistic … calculations gave him enough to complete three laps non-stop.'

The same paper's editorial pages begged to differ. 'Maybe,' they thundered, 'if Honda had spent as much time on working out the fuel consumption for a rider who always goes faster in a TT than in practice, instead of thinking of self-embarrassing protests, the result might have been different.'

To add to Joey's woes, he got home to discover he'd been burgled. 'The beds were ripped and the wardrobes emptied. All my trophies had been turned out, but they weren't stolen. All that was missing was about £350 in cash.'

In many ways the TT protest and its unfortunate aftermath summed up a disappointing year. Crosby once again took the world Formula One championship, also winning every round of the British series in which he finished. Joey placed third, behind Haslam, but even at Dundrod could manage no better than fifth in the feature event. True, their bikes weren't perfect. Ron, in particular, was critical of both the speed and handling of his RCB Honda. But what on earth had happened to the Joey of old?

For much of the season he was away from friends and family, contesting the UK Formula One and Streetbike series. He finished a disappointing sixth in both. Home was either his van, a flat provided by Honda in Chiswick, or the Haslams' guest room. 'Joey and Ron were much the same,' explained Symmons. 'When Joe was doing F1 races in England, Anne and Ron took good care of him, made sure he had his breakfast. The two of them were very alike. They had a lot of mutual respect and a great relationship as team-mates.'

Yet still Himself was not happy. As Davy Wood recalls, 'Here he was, a works rider, in a team with Gardner and Haslam, around 22 staff, factory bikes and mechanics, but he was way out of his environment. In September I got a call to go to Brands Hatch, where I found Joey not at all happy. "It's all right," he said, "but it's not for me."

'Gerald Davidson asked me what had happened to the guy he'd signed. I told him if he'd lend him back to me, and a few motorcycles, I'd lend him back the old Joey for the Formula One series. And that, more or less, is what Honda did.' After rounding off the season with a couple of holiday rides in Macau and South Africa, Joey went back to his roots.

Luckily – although it didn't seem so at the time – Davy had rounded off his own racing season when he 'took a bad toss and broke both my legs badly. So Joey said, "Look, will you do the talking and I'll do the riding?", and that's how it started.

'For 1982 they gave us a 250 and a 1000, I got some backing from Downtown Radio, and that year we won 32 races. In 1984 DAF trucks were also on board, plus we had a 500.' At last the boys were going places, Irish style.

1982

No coins were minted to mark the start of Joey's 1982 campaign, although he did begin the season by passing his motorcycle road test in Coleraine. Henceforth any unofficial testing of race bikes on Antrim's country lanes would not be quite so illegal as before. He also signed

Tools, tabs and transport. Joey takes a break in his truck. For nourishment Joey's standard diet was beans, but at Macau Barry Symmons once saw him presented with a couple of local delicacies – a chicken's head and a 1000-year-old egg. Joey scoffed both. (Stephen Davison – Pacemaker)

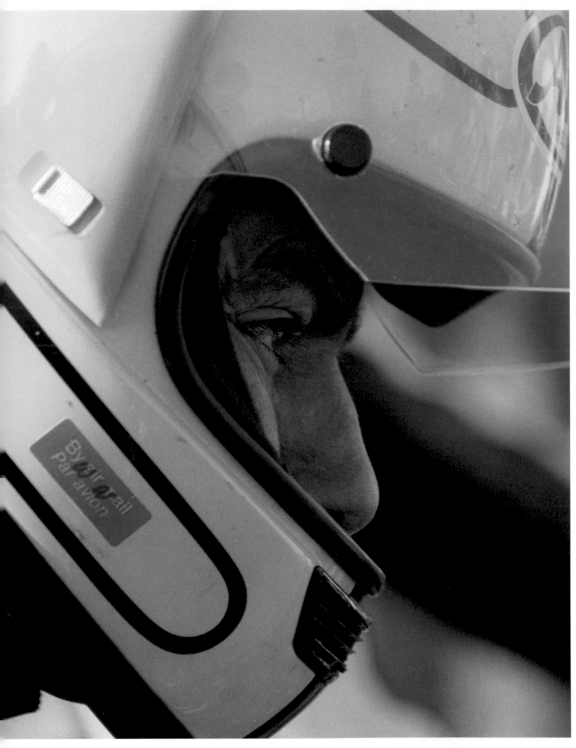

Before the start: utterly focused and ready to fly. (Stephen Davison – Pacemaker)

possibly his busiest season on UK short circuits, contesting the British TT F1 championship and a few rounds of the *Motor Cycle News* Superbike series on his 999 Honda four, as well as the Shell Oils Streetbike series on a CB1100R.

In the Streetbike championship he looked set to win the final round at Brands Hatch, but slid off painfully at Bottom Bend, leaving Wayne Gardner to win both the race and the championship. Ron Haslam placed second, with Joey third in a Honda clean sweep. Roger Marshall won the domestic Formula One series (and practically everything else) for Suzuki, with Joey in sixth place.

On the roads, of course, it was a different matter, although this was far from Joey's most emphatic year. At May's North-West 200, in a meeting blighted by John Newbold's death, Mick Grant edged Joey into second place, whilst third-placed Rob McElnea posted notice of the threat he would become in setting a fastest lap at 123.66mph.

For the first time, the world Formula One series expanded to include a non-UK round although hostilities began, as usual, on the Isle of Man in June. Joey's main opposition came from team-mate Ron Haslam and the Suzuki veteran Mick Grant. After posting a new lap record on the opening lap, Grant retired when his engine died, leaving Haslam to sweep by at Ramsey Hairpin and inherit the lead. Having blown up his best engine in the final practice session, Joey was beset by handling problems and a bike that wouldn't rev beyond 9000rpm. He finished second, over 4½ minutes in arrears.

Although irrelevant to Joey's World Championship ambitions, the Classic TT was an even bigger shambles. It proved to be a race of attrition won by Ireland only in the form of the unfancied Kiwi – Dennis – of that name. Joey had been due to ride one of the latest V-four Hondas, but was relieved when the team switched back to the old 1024cc straight fours when the new machine broke its swing-arm landing heavily at Ballaugh Bridge in the final practice session. 'It's incredibly quick but we need more time to

his first personal sponsorship contract, with Top Tek helmets of Stranraer.

Although now based in Ireland, Joey had

prepare it for the TT,' he explained. 'On Sulby Straight I had to knock it off because of the handling.'

Riding the old straight four he led early on, but the bike gradually slowed, dropping him to sixth on lap five when his chain snapped at the Bungalow. Haslam fared no better, retiring at the pits with a huge oil leak. As privateer Ireland brought his RG500 to an improbable win, Chas Mortimer's newspaper column slated the 'appalling reliability' of the factory machines. Perhaps fittingly, Hesketh Motorcycles went bust that same week.

Vila Real was next. The baking July heat of Northern Portugal brought one of the surprises of the year when 23-year-old Wayne Gardner won over 25 laps of the daunting street circuit, an impressively gutsy performance. With Haslam busy elsewhere, Joey eased to another second place which meant that fourth place in the final round at Dundrod would guarantee him the world title.

At the Ulster Grand Prix Joey wisely opted out of a ferocious battle between Honda team-mate Haslam and the Suzuki of Norman Brown which saw Brown crash out on the final lap. When Mick Grant's crank broke at Tournagrough, 'Himself' was promoted to second. Joey's third runner-up slot in as many rounds was comfortably enough to make him the first Irishman since Ralph Bryans in 1965 to clinch a world crown – and a mighty celebration that left half the province nursing a thick head the next day.

Joey Dunlop, champion of the world. It sounded good. Not that he'd get carried away, then or in the future.

To a man such as Joey, being a works star and World Champion wasn't the be-all and end-all. Simply enjoying racing and soaking in the craic mattered at least as much. A tale from Jim Dunlop speaks volumes: 'Joey came back after racing on the Continent one time, desperate for a "proper" race on the roads. I was entered at Aghadowey, so I practised on the 350, then he swapped into my leathers and helmet in the back of the van, and went out on my bike as me. I think he finished

about seventh, but obviously he had to take it easy 'cos he couldn't afford to get on the rostrum.'

This is how many flies sacrifice themselves for a typical TT win at around 120mph. (Don Morley)

The Unbeatable Alliance

'What a fantastic ride … in a class of his own … he makes everyone else look slow'
Wayne Gardner, after watching Joey hurtle down Bray Hill

By 1986 Joey and 'Reg' Marshall rode for opposing factories, but their rivalry was probably less intense than when they were team-mates two years before. (Clifford McLean)

It's doubtful whether Honda truly appreciated what they were doing when they agreed to leave Joey to his own devices. Factory teams simply don't farm out their hardware and reputations so readily as that, especially when the factory in question is the largest and most image-conscious on earth. It was an arrangement unique in modern motorsport.

1983

Honda had other things on their corporate mind too. In anticipation of a 750cc limit on Formula One engines from the following year, Honda's main effort in 1983 focused on an 850cc version of a new breed of V-four. Other than Formula One championship races, Joey's contract now allowed him to run the previous year's factory bikes in his own race team. The arrangement worked well. 'Before I had to take a back seat. Now what I say goes,' he observed, clearly relishing his new independence. If this unusual state of affairs caused anyone concern, it didn't seem to trouble Joey and the boys. One of the first things they did was throw away Honda's expensively-developed chassis and install one of their own.

'It was the first year he'd been let loose on his own,' recalls Curly Scott, 'and he had the F1 bike with Downtown sponsorship. He never was happy with the handling, so I built a new frame for the 1000cc four. We more or less picked up the [reference] points off the steel chassis, but made it in ally and strengthened it where it seemed to need it. It wasn't a pretty thing, but Joey liked it right off when he tested it at Kirkistown.'

Factory riders had been sacked for such heresy, and heaven knows what Honda made of it. As Rob McElnea remarked many years later: 'What sort of factory set-up is it that lets a rider put their engine in his own frame?' The answer, of course, is any set-up in which Joey makes up the rules.

Nor was Irish enterprise confined to the frame. 'The first race was at Donington,' continues Curly. 'We'd also bumped up the compression to run avgas, but had to borrow the right jets off the Honda Britain boys. Of course then the bike flew. Gardner didn't like it, and they took the jets back. Joey didn't like that at all. He led the race but wasn't allowed to win it – he just sat up on the finish straight, really obvious, and let him pass.'

Over the years Joey would develop a network of mates who could fabricate all manner of special parts. In Ballymoney-speak, these were 'him midgen' – home made ones. Curly created one-off bits for Joey for the rest of his career, often with little regard for Honda's own engineering notions. 'I remember once with the V-four, it had this powerful heavy bearing housing, so I got my brother Jim to make a copy in light ally. Later that year we went to Silverstone, and Honda took the bikes off us to prep 'em for the race. When we got 'em back all our bits were missing.'

Team Ballymoney's talent for bodging would become legendary. Willie describes later problems with a 500cc triple at the Skerries road races, near Dublin. A slot in the selector drum had broken, jamming the gearbox. 'We had the notion of drilling the drum and putting in a bolt to replace the missing bit. It was hardened steel so took ages, with a hand drill. But eventually I tapped the hole, fitted a screw and filed it clean. It worked a treat for the rest of the season. That bike went back to Japan like that and I often wonder what they made of it.'

On the face of it, campaigning an RS850 against the 997cc Suzukis placed Honda at a grave disadvantage in 1983, despite rumours of 11,500rpm and 135bhp. Initially the V-four was no match for the big Suzukis – nor even for the previous year's 998cc Honda straight fours which both Dunlop and new team-mate Roger

Marshall used for some English short-circuit meetings. Although the RS had more ground clearance, stopped and handled better and had good top-end speed, it lacked the bigger engines' punch out of turns. Nonetheless,

Mechanic Dave Sleat readies Joey's 850 Honda for the Senior Classic in 1983. Joey and Norman Brown set The Island ablaze but Rob McElnea won. (Don Morley)

Wayne Gardner would use the 850 in every round for which it was available to capture the British ACU TT Formula One crown.

As if in keeping with the theme of novelty, Joey arrived on The Island that May with a beard, and would later be joined by his new son, Gary, born the Saturday before. The other new baby – Honda's RS850 – had already shown promise on the roads after winning first time out at the North-West 200. But, limited to a single decent lap by 'lots of wee machine problems and the diabolical weather', he could manage only sixth on the TT leaderboard, almost 3mph slower than Rob McElnea. 'But everything that went wrong was simple to put right,' he added, 'and I always seem to do better in races when I've had a bad practice.'

When the final Friday session was called off,

Joey did a last 'practice' lap in John Rea's Ford Escort. 'I drove the course from 1.00am to 4.00am working out where my braking points should be and so on. That's when it all finally comes together. We set the bike up at Jurby in the afternoon and I went to bed feeling very confident.'

If any one race marked the start of The King of the Roads' reign, the 1983 Formula One TT was it. Taking 8.2 seconds off Mick Grant's lap record from a standing start, Joey simply blitzed the race. Although a wheel change briefly put Grant back in the lead after lap four, such was the superiority of Himself and the RS850 that he still won by 53 seconds at record race speed.

'That was the hardest race of my life,' he gasped afterwards, but the RS850 'could have

Joey at Assen in 1983 – one of Rob McElnea's most memorable wins, but it couldn't stop Joey landing the world title. (Don Morley)

been purpose-built for The Island. Giving away 150cc it probably isn't the fastest, but it lets you make use of all the power it's got. When I'd pulled out a 30-second or so lead I eased off. I could have gone quicker but there's no point if you don't have to.'

Leading on all six laps gained Joey £10,250 in prize money, a record for a TT race. He could afford to celebrate with a few 'swallows', as Barry Symmons just about remembers: 'We all went to the Irish Embassy to celebrate. I remember Willie singing the Londonderry Air, which was his party piece. Then Joey decided he was going to get me drunk – on Black Bush. My legs gave way on the way back to the Esplanade Hotel, I crawled up the stairs, and crashed head-first into the dinner gong. It was 3.30am and I woke most of the hotel.'

Linda, not for the last time, missed her husband's triumph. 'After having Gary they wouldn't let me out of hospital until Formula One day,' she complained, 'because they knew I'd be going there as soon as they did. Joey won the Formula One and I flew over on the Tuesday with Gary. Joey always went for two weeks. I'd normally fly on the Thursday of practice week with Ernie Coates' wife, her four children and my five – plus maybe an engine for Joey. And tyres, there were always tyres. It was a nightmare. But we really enjoyed it.'

If the Formula One was a triumph, the Classic TT was a mess. A heavier fuel load transformed the V-four into an ill-handling 'monster … a completely different bike … on the second lap it wouldn't run on more than three cylinders until the bumps released the breather pipe'. Looking at the Honda's broken screen, Joey added, 'I spent more time on top of the screen than underneath it'.

Although Rob McElnea won, another Irishman was hero that day. Norman Brown, a Newry publican's son, set a staggering 115.24mph standing-start lap on Hector Neill's RG500, only to run out of fuel on lap three, leaving him coasting at Kate's.

In the crowd that day at the 11th Milestone, an ultra-fast right-left bend, was a young Scottish racer on his first visit to the Isle of

Perhaps not The King's natural territory: riding the 500cc triple at the British Grand Prix, Silverstone, 1984. (Phil Masters)

Man. 'When Norman and Joey came through,' Steve Hislop remembers, 'I nearly fell backwards off the bank in surprise. Boy, look at that! It was that moment that made me want to do it too. And lo and behold, five years later I was Joey's team-mate.' In September 1983 Steve's Manx career began with second place in the 250cc Newcomers race. The winner, coincidentally, was none other than wee Robert Dunlop.

The Classic TT was a disappointment, but only World Formula One points really mattered. At the Dutch TT, McElnea won, with Joey second. 'We had a fantastic race on the old Assen circuit,' remembers Rob Mac of one of his most memorable dices. 'I did him on the last lap, in front of 200,000 people. Mega, one of the biggest things in my career.'

Going into the final round at the Ulster Grand Prix, Joey led McElnea by a slender two points and Honda pulled out all the stops. A special aluminium-framed 920cc big-bore version of the RS850 was shipped from Japan just 10 days before the race and tested at

He rode harder and braver than anyone else

Opposite: *Joey leads Wayne Gardner who leads Reg Marshall during the Formula One support race at the 1984 British GP. Gardner won.* (Don Morley)

'He'd work half the night on his bikes … he loved the garage to himself.' (Stephen Davison – Pacemaker)

Kirkistown. Practice at Dundrod was in sunshine, but when it rained on race day Joey showed that he had little need of Honda's extra capacity. McElnea and Grant led off the line, but Joey hurtled past the pair of them into Rushyhill corner and wasn't seen again by either until the rostrum. The title was his, by 42 points to McElnea's 35.

'I was on pole, Joey second, and I thought I could win,' remembers McElnea. 'Then it pissed down. I got the hole-shot, down what they call 'the flying kilometre' to the first corner, which is quick – nearly flat in the dry. Joey came past me with his knee on the ground, and just disappeared. I looked round at Mick Grant and just put my hands up. Every lap after that I got the "wanker" sign from about 30 Joey fans in a lay-by.'

If Joey's first world title was a less than emphatic affair, this time respect was clearly due. In the trickiest of conditions he rode harder and braver than anyone else was prepared to go – and they all knew it. Joey was The Man.

1984

New to the Honda Britain team for 1983 had been Roger 'Reg' Marshall, a superb rider on both short and road circuits. Having served his Honda apprenticeship supporting Joey, Marshall now had loftier ambitions. 'This was the year I wanted to take over,' he explained. 'If you became Formula One champ you were Honda's main man, and I had my sights on that.' It was going to be head-to-head: the gregarious and popular Englishman against Ireland's publicity-shy folk hero.

'Roger was underrated but really adaptable,' reckoned Honda mechanic Nick Goodison. 'He seemed to be able to ride anything on any sort of circuit. And for him, winning the Formula

One title would have opened more doors than Joey was interested in walking through.'

But first, there was the road race season opener to negotiate. One of the main problems with the early V-fours was carburation flat spots, which were so bad at the North-West 200 that the Honda squad ran out of official practice time. 'So we went back to Joey's,' recalls Goodison, 'and carried on testing on the road outside his house – blatting up and down, absolutely flat-out, until it was almost dark. Crazy. Roger was "mysteriously" ill and Wayne [Gardner] wasn't into it, so Joey rode everyone's bike to set it up, which I thought was fantastic. He really wanted to help the team.'

As it turned out, Joey's selfless effort was largely wasted as he retired from both the main race and the 250cc event. Graham Wood took the feature race, the only one run in the dry. Joey had some consolation in going to the top of the *MCN* Masters championship standings by taking double points in winning his 'home' round – despite a bike that misfired throughout. Marshall capped a miserable weekend when he crashed out spectacularly at Portrush's Dhu Varen corner.

'Maybe that's the bad luck out of the way before the TT,' said Joey. Formula One apart, he couldn't have been more wrong. With the new 750cc limit, only Honda were ever going to be in the hunt in the five-round series, having campaigned a broadly similar machine in 1983. The TT showed the task facing Suzuki.

Joey won, with a record lap at almost 116mph, but not without problems of his own. On lap three he stopped in a cloud of blue smoke at Braddan, then again at Union Mills. 'I got off and parked her against the hedge. I thought the rear wheel had jammed, gave her a kick then noticed that the exhaust pipe was jamming against the tyre.' Joey later offered an apology to the two young lads who'd offered him a push-start, an act which he knew would see him disqualified. In the heat of the moment he 'maybe told them to "go away" or words to that effect, but they were only trying to help. Anyway, they got the burst tail pipe as a souvenir … I'll autograph it for them some time.'

'By then I wasn't in the best frame of mind … crabbit and angry … it took me at least half a lap to get back into a rhythm.' Joey had seen a 50-second lead become a 24-second deficit to Marshall, suffering exhaust and fuel problems of his own, and only that lap record regained him the lead. It was a race Honda seemed desperate to lose, but luckily for them Suzuki were trying even harder. Grant's Suzuki gearbox broke, and McElnea's trashed its steering damper and then seized.

Joey got to bed at 4.30am after celebrating and reminiscing with Ernie Coates and Norman Dunne about another great day for Ireland and for Himself. Six days later there was less to celebrate, as Rob McElnea made it back-to-back Senior wins after a furious battle at lap record speeds.

Riding the RG500 Suzuki McElnea lapped at 118.23 – fully 2mph up on the old mark. Joey responded to such impertinence by breaking the lap record on every one of the first five laps and held a comfortable 40-second lead with less than 10 miles to go. Then the 500cc triple 'started to rattle and slow down' and coasted impotently to a halt at Mountain Hut.

Although there were claims of a broken crankshaft, the reality seemed far simpler. In the heat of battle, Joey had stopped for fuel after three laps, instead of four, having already stopped after lap two: 'I just got confused about which lap I was on because my visor and screen were covered in flies and I couldn't see the signals'. Astonishingly, he ran out of fuel in almost the same place to lose the Junior race. Fuel again proved decisive when McElnea ran the six-lap Premier Classic race on one pit stop to Joey's two.

If the potential rivalry between Joey and Reg Marshall had been subdued so far, it resurfaced at the Dutch TT, held on the new Assen circuit. At 3.8 miles this was almost one mile less than the previous track, and far less road-like in character. Joey led until the fuel stop in the 25-

Opposite: Cranked over through Parliament Square in the 1984 Junior TT, before retiring on the final lap for the second time that week. Note sponsorship from Ernie Coates, one of Joey's many faithful followers. (Don Morley)

After annihilating the Mountain Circuit record with a lap at 118.47mph on the 500-3, engine failure robs Joey of the 1984 Senior TT. (Don Morley)

lap race when lightning pit-work gave Marshall a lead he would hold until the flag. Having set the fastest lap of the race, Reg won by 13 seconds.

When he learned that much of Marshall's speed in the pits came from not stopping his engine – a clear breach of race regulations – Joey was livid. However, Symmons wasn't about to jeopardise a Honda one-two by protesting his own man. After a lengthy bout of

behind-the-scenes jiggery-pokery, Yugoslavian rider Mile Pajic was persuaded to protest instead, but by then his case was rejected as being out of time. Marshall's win stood, tying the Honda duo for the championship lead.

At Vila Real, held in searing temperatures, Marshall needed no pit-stop short cuts. His fitness training – four days a week with Grimsby Town football club – paid off, whilst Joey's more laid-back approach did not. When

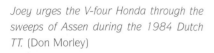

Joey urges the V-four Honda through the sweeps of Assen during the 1984 Dutch TT. (Don Morley)

he finished, over a minute behind Marshall, he had to be lifted from his bike in a heat-stricken daze. Symmons took his place on the rostrum.

There would be no such climatic problems at the next round, the Ulster Grand Prix – just more heat for Symmons. At Windmill Corner on the last lap, Joey dived under Marshall to take the lead, holding on to the win by 2.6 seconds. Reg was apoplectic. The manoeuvre was 'lunatic'. He demanded that Symmons protest his team-mate for dangerous riding. Joey shrugged: 'We didn't touch … I just don't think Roger expected the pass.'

Either way, if Symmons hadn't protested Marshall in neutral Holland, he was scarcely about to protest Ireland's favourite son in his own back yard. Wisely, he let the result be. Even so, the Honda truck was vandalised and both he and Marshall were abused by Irish fans convinced of an English bias. (Ironically Symmons later married an Irish lass and now lives in Belfast.)

Marshall is much more sanguine about the incident now. 'I went into Windmill as hard as I ever had, but Joey came under me as I was fully committed. I had to pick the bike up, so hit the bank on the way out – had to cog down two gears to get going again. By then he was long gone. I was pretty pumped up, obviously, and wound up too. But I calmed down later. When we got to [the final round at] Zolder I shook Joey's hand and said "let the best man win."'

Reg wasn't the only one with that aspiration. The team – and several hundred unofficial Irish 'stewards' intent on seeing fair play – journeyed to Zolder knowing that nothing could prevent a Honda one-two. But in which order? The answer was anticlimactic. One third of the way through the 36-lap race Marshall's bike slowed, allowing Joey to take the lead and pull away. When Reg pitted his crew could find nothing wrong and sent him out again, only for his V-four to expire at the end of the pit lane in a cloud of steam. The head gasket had blown. Joey just had to finish to take the title, and he cruised into second place behind Pajic's Kawasaki.

'It was raining at Zolder,' remembers Roger Burnett, 'which was to Joey's advantage. But

Roger was on a high, and had been all week. He'd kept wanting to do all sorts of daft things to psyche Joey out, like taking cold showers in the middle of the night – and it was bloody cold. In qualifying he looked good. Mind you, Roger never was that sympathetic to his engines.' Ironically the cause of the breakdown seems to have lain with mechanic Chris Mayhew's obsession with getting things right. When he'd stripped the V-four to check it before the race, he'd innocently replaced the cylinder head gasket with a new one from a faulty batch.

It was an unsatisfactory outcome for both riders, and a crushing disappointment to Marshall whose championship campaign ended, literally, in tears in Roger Burnett's caravan. For Joey, triumph was muted. 'I'd rather have won fair and square, but that's racing,' he said, before prophesying that 'next year it'll be different. I can't see Honda holding that much superiority forever'. He was right. The next year's dominance would be more crushing still.

Joey was livid about losing to team-mate Reg Marshall at Assen in June 1984, but wrapped up the world title in Belgium a couple of months later. (Don Morley)

Water, Water Everywhere

*'Norman Dunne rang me about 6am, shouting something about a boat going down.
I told him he was pissed and put the phone down.'*

Journalist Norrie White on being offered the scoop on the sinking of the 'Tornammona'

Opposite: *Joey Dunlop and the Honda RVF750.* (Don Morley)

Joey, in new Savile Row blazer, tells Chris Searle why – apart from free smokes – signing for Rothmans was such a good deal. (Don Morley)

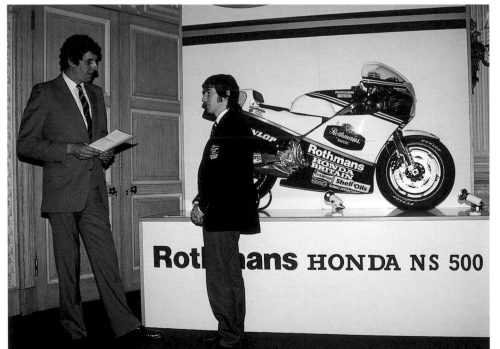

The 1985 season brought Rothmans' mighty budget to the Honda team and what new team member Roger Burnett described as 'a completely new level of sponsorship, really special'. In order to indoctrinate the team in Rothmans ways, everyone – riders, managers and mechanics – were obliged to attend a corporate seminar. 'They took us all to this hotel near Aylesbury. To me, Joey was a star, but he looked like a fish out of water. When we'd signed up they sent us all to Austin Reed in Savile Row to get measured for a blazer. Joey looked like he'd sent someone else to get fitted for his. His one advantage was that he smoked like a chimney. Him and Barry Symmons seemed to get through the whole team's cigarette allocation on their own.'

1985

Big bucks budget or not, Joey had already begun 1985 as officially Britain's most celebrated rider, having won both the *Motor Cycle News* and Enkalon Irish 'Man of the Year' on the basis of popular polls. He was equally fêted among manufacturers but, having turned down an offer from Suzuki, he remained Honda's man – and wisely so, as he would be paired with arguably the finest four-stroke racing machine ever built. The bike was the RVF750, and it would give Joey his most emphatic World Championship win.

Nick Goodison was the mechanic Honda Britain despatched to Japan to learn about and assemble the exquisite little RVF750. Only three such bikes were built that year. Honda France had two for endurance racing, and Joey was granted a 'sprint' version for his World Formula One defence.

Its first British outing was the North-West 200 in May, where Joey sped to an easy double win. 'It was gorgeous,' cooed Nick, 'so tiny and so fast. We wheeled it across the field to the scrutineering tent and it looked like it belonged in a different race than everything else. Rob Mac was there, in his heyday on the Skoal Bandit Suzuki, but Joey just pissed off.

'He absolutely loved the bike from Day One. It was a proper race bike – almost everything else was a converted road bike. And it was so good, you barely had to change the settings wherever you went, although we had Ron Williams, and a Showa technician, at most F1 rounds. And everyone put in a big effort. Dunlop [tyres] made a huge commitment. They made Joey his own tyres, with 'JD' moulded into the sides.

'We won every round of the World Championship. I don't think anyone bothered him all year.'

For Roger Marshall and Joey the tribulations, not to say rivalries, of the previous Formula One campaign seemed to be forgotten. When the pair weren't sharing bikes in endurance races, they'd often share the same hotel room. 'We got on very well together,' Reg recalls. 'I think I was one of the few racers who really did. A lot of people thought they knew him, but not many did. He was such a loner.'

Goodison echoes the remark. 'I used to drive the truck, along with another mechanic on a rota. Joey was a real loner. He'd set off on his own, sometimes weeks before the race, and eventually just front up. He'd be relaxed and up for it, and it worked well. After the race we'd pack up and go our separate ways. We rarely tested, so we'd just meet up at the next round. It was perfect.'

Regrettably this perfection in transport did not extend to Joey's customary fishing boat trip to The Island. 'The first I heard about the shipwreck was when Mel Murphy rang,' explained Linda.

'Don't panic,' Mel began, 'but the boat's sunk.'

'I'll never forget those words. And what's the first thing I did? Panic, of course.'

There were 13 on board Archie Lappin's converted fishing boat *Tornammona* when she went down in 70 feet of water after hitting rocks a mile out of Portaferry en route to Peel. Belfast coastguards received the distress call at 12:17am.

'I think we had problems to do with the change in currents,' grins Andy Inglis. 'There was a sudden crunch and we sank very quickly.'

Robert remembers that the boat 'just ground to a halt, sitting on the rocks … the real hairy part was when we were on the rocks and couldn't get off for the white water. The incredible thing

was that no-one was ever in the water – just straight into the life-rafts.' The evacuation was timed by coastguards at 11 minutes.

Joey, who was frying chops when the boat struck the rocks, distinguished himself by calmly taking a penknife to the painter of the life raft, which the *Tornammona* was threatening to drag under the waves. Both frying pan and penknife would later enjoy pride of place in Joey's Bar.

The rescue operation involved lifeboats from Portaferry and Donaghadee and a RAF helicopter. Eight bikes sank with the boat, including the EMC on which Robert Dunlop had just won at Cookstown, Brian Reid's new 500

Opposite: *Suzuka 8-hours, 1986, Joey and Reg Marshall rode the infamous Little White Bull. 'A joke, ridiculously slow' reckoned Reg.* (Stephen Davison – Pacemaker)

Joey and Mel Murphy in pensive mood. Big Mel was the wind in the sails of the Armoy Armada but died tragically young in 1986. (Clifford McLean)

Spondon Yam, Sam McClements' 750 and Noel Hudson's three machines. Luckily for Joey, the only machine he had on board was a 250cc dirt bike. But the Jimmy Simpson trophy, awarded to Joey for his lap record in 1984, was also lost.

Divers led by bike fan Alan Brown worked to salvage the sunken bikes, and the trophy. 'It was amazing how quickly things corroded,' remembers Robert, 'even though we washed off the salt and steeped the bikes overnight in a bath of diesel.'

Reaction on the Isle of Man was mixed. Barry Symmons didn't know that Joey's race bikes had gone by commercial ferry, so when he heard of the sinking he presumed the worst. When journalist Norrie White took the opposite view, that even by Irish standards the yarn was too far-fetched to be true, *Motor Cycle News* nearly missed the story: 'Norman Dunne rang me about 6.00am, shouting something about a boat going down. I told him he was pissed and put the phone down.'

Joey eventually flew to The Island on the Monday, and proceeded to prove that the worse a TT fortnight begins, the better it

finishes. In the Formula One race his winning margin from Tony Rutter's second-placed Suzuki was fully five minutes and 40 seconds – or about 11 miles.

If the opening race was utterly dominant, victory in the Junior race owed much to good luck. Brian Reid led for most of the race, taking a 14-second advantage into the last lap before running out of petrol. 'I saw Brian stopped just after Hillberry on the last lap – it must have been heartbreaking for him,' Joey said of his old adversary from the Dromara Destroyers.

Rather than ride the 500 triple in the Senior, Joey elected to ride the RVF once again. 'He was always a bit dubious about riding the 500,' said Nick Goodison, 'because the four-strokes had the edge in reliability and stability.' The decision brought Joey what he described as 'one of the easiest rides I've had on The Island' and a record-equalling third TT win in one week.

Little over one month later, Reg and Joey found themselves in Japan for the Suzuka 8-hours, then the world's biggest bike race. Although Ron Haslam and Alex George placed second in 1979, and Marshall partnered Ron to sixth place a year later, the 8-hour has rarely given British riders much joy. Honda owned the Suzuka circuit, but even here being a multiple World Champion didn't always get its due reward. The duo were to ride something dubbed 'The Little White Bull' for Soichiro Honda's son in a race won by Gardner and Tokuno's full-on RVF. 'It was a joke, ridiculously slow,' sneered Reg about the bike. 'Joey was livid. He got straight on the phone to Barry Symmons, but had to ride it in the end.'

'It had a CBX750 engine – an across-the-frame four – and was dead slow,' recalls Nick Goodison. 'Roger was flat on the tank trying to crawl under the paint, and someone went past him sat bolt upright. But it was on this trip that Joey first saw the RC30 prototype. He was pretty excited by that.'

If Suzuka was a futile waste of an air-fare, the Formula One season would give Joey his most emphatic championship success. Joey slaughtered them, winning all six rounds on the RVF750. Only at Assen was he pushed. On a tricky, drying track, Joey led by 31 seconds until his fuel stop. Mick Grant, needing no stop, closed, and was a mere 0.3 seconds behind at the end. Marshall's bad luck continued when his bike dropped a valve for the second race in succession.

Vila Real, run in typically crippling temperatures, brought another unfortunate watery incident. At the finish the pit lane resembled a field hospital, with riders collapsed in various stages of heat exhaustion. As Joey headed for his pit after taking the chequered flag, local rider Manual Joao raced out of his in a sorry attempt to qualify as a finisher. For one horrible moment it appeared that he might T-bone the incoming, exhausted Joey. Spotting this, Barry Symmons hurled a water bottle at the Portuguese rider, hitting him on the shoulder and causing him to clip the kerb and crash. Joao leaped to his feet, ran back and kicked his assailant, soon aided by his mechanics.

Attempts to exclude Joey from the results foundered when video evidence supported Symmons' actions. After sustaining three cracked ribs and a good kicking on behalf of his rider, Symmons ruefully observed, 'I think Joey realised that I probably had his interests at heart, providing I wasn't wearing a tie'.

But if Portugal was bad, Barcelona was far worse. It was the first Formula One round to be held at Montjuich Park, a road circuit accustomed to putting on notoriously ill-organised 24-hour races. Joey had just taken the lead on lap 15 when fourth-placed Andy McGladdery's engine blew, spewing oil across the track. Domingo Pares, Ray Swann and Tony Rutter all went down on the oil, the latter with serious injuries. Even one lap later, with a medic attending to Rutter, the only marshalling appeared to be the hapless McGladdery's frantic arm-waving. Somehow Joey sneaked through the carnage but McGregor, Juan Garriga and Nat Wood all crashed amidst the chaos. Although reigning Formula Two champion Rutter survived, he would never fully recover from his injuries. Joey cruised to a sorry win and became champion one week later with the cancellation of the Zolder round.

The next round might have been a mournful

*Nowhere did Joey show his determination
more than at Portugal's gruelling Vila
Real street circuit, winning in 1985 and
1986 in blistering heat.* (Stephen
Davison – Pacemaker)

**He said the
Daimler had
about as much
room in the back
as his van did**

anticlimax had it been held anywhere but
Dundrod. As it was, the Irish had a double
celebration as Joey cruised majestically to this
third successive world crown, with Brian Reid
claiming his first Formula Two title. Ironically,
the former Destroyer crashed and broke his
thigh barely half an hour later. But nothing
could halt Joey's progress, as he went on to
record win number six at Germany's
Hockenheimring.

When they came to the final tally, Joey had
90 points, fully 50 more than runner-up Mick
Grant. Writing in *Motocourse*, the annual
racing 'bible', Nick Harris described Joey as
'the greatest pure road racer of all time'. The
same article regretted the lack of recognition
his exploits received in what the English like to
call 'the mainland'. What more did he have to
do to prove his mettle?

1986

If Joey failed to gain the appreciation he
deserved in a few backwaters, Buckingham

Palace was not one of them, for this was the
year The King of the Roads was honoured by
the Queen. When the New Year honours were
released, there, listed under the MBEs, was
William Joseph Dunlop.

'The Queen meant a great deal to Joey, so
this was important to him,' remembers Barry
Symmons. 'He was immaculate, and Linda
wouldn't have been out of place at Ascot. The
whole family was a picture. We sent them off to
the palace in a Daimler, which he reckoned had
almost as much room in the back as his van.'

After that, there was another title to be won.
Perversely, as Formula One prepared to give
way to World Superbikes, the series found itself
with better fields at more rounds on more
varied circuits than ever before. But for all the
changes, and despite early shocks, it was to
prove business as usual for Joey.

The first surprise, dubbed Joey's 'Misano
Disaster', came in the opening round on 6
April. Joey's strategy of changing tyres during a
rain-affected race appeared to have paid off, as
he tailed Marco Lucchinelli's ailing, sliding

Joey shares a lap of honour with two of racing's extroverts, Marco Lucchinelli (left) and Fred Merkel, at the 1988 British World Superbike round. (Phil Masters)

Ducati into the final lap. Having hauled in the Italian by over a second a lap on the previous 20, he was just about to pounce when the Honda spluttered and ran out of fuel. Only Lucchinelli and Andersson completed the full 160-mile race distance and, with not a single British rider in the top eight, it was one of the strangest F1 results of all time.

At Hockenheim four weeks later, Joey was left on the line adjusting his knee sliders as the rest of the pack left the grid. Twentieth as he headed into the forests for the first time, his RVF was seventh after lap one, second after two and leading one tour later. After pitting mid race he hauled in Paul Iddon's Suzuki, established an eight-second lead and held it there to the flag. It was a masterful short circuit display by the road race specialist.

Assen brought yet another cock-up, this time long after Joey inherited the win when the chain of Neil Robinson's Suzuki jammed. Returning from their victory celebrations, a lap of the circuit seemed to be in order for the Honda crew. Unfortunately mechanic Dave

Sleat was not so adept as Joey at keeping on the grey stuff, and all seven occupants were lucky to escape with their lives when he put their car into a ditch at the third turn. As well as suffering five broken ribs and a sprained ankle, Joey needed stitches above his left eye when he was hit on the head by the marble base of the trophy he'd just won for more conventional lappery.

The crash left Joey in no condition for the punishing heat of Jerez, where he slipped to fifth behind Paul Iddon's increasingly threatening Suzuki. With Iddon now on a mission, the heat of Vila Real loomed ominously just one week later.

Iddon remembers it well. 'It was 118 degrees on the grid, and they kept us waiting there for about 20 minutes. When it started Joey cleared off. It was horrible – sweat pouring off you, stinging your eyes ... your head just wanted to explode. Then my signals started telling me I was catching Joey – fast. He was obviously suffering badly, but I made the mistake of passing him as soon as I reached him. He dug deep and passed me back, too late to do anything about it. Looking back, you realise how wily he was – he always seemed to have something extra to call on, even when he was struggling.' That extra something was a new lap record, 1.5 seconds inside the old mark, set in a state of near collapse.

'My other memory,' says Iddon, 'is not being able to understand him. I spent more time with his entourage, who seemed to spend their lives trying to get me drunk, especially the night before a race. Joey often kept his distance – I suppose he had to. After Vila Real, we all drank the hotel practically dry. I went to bed late, but when I got up they were still at it – on the last bottle of crème de menthe. The whole crowd of 'em used to travel around in this old blue Mercedes van, with a vodka optic in the back. But Joey kept himself to himself. He was very quiet – when you've got extroverts like Fred Merkel in the paddock, you don't tend to notice the likes of Joey.'

Donington Park, 1988: Paul Iddon chases Joey out of Goddards Hairpin in the race in which Carl Fogarty grabbed his first world title. (Honda Europe/Phil Masters)

A further win at Imatra gave Joey an unassailable 20-point lead, which was just as well as a wrong tyre choice in the wet blighted his chances at Dundrod. Robinson won impressively, but joy was to be tragically short-lived: three weeks later he was killed racing at Scarborough. Then came Big Mel Murphy's death from a heart attack.

Shortly after, the TT was preening itself as the Duke of Kent opened the present grandstand, replacing the wooden contraption erected in 1926. More remarkably still, this was the TT where not one but two Dunlops crashed. Robert slid off his Yamaha at Cronk Urleigh in Tuesday's Formula Two race, breaking seven ribs, an ankle, and shoulder, and puncturing a lung. Joey pulled out of the first Production race to be with his brother, who was in intensive care until Friday. Unthinkably, Joey himself crashed at Sulby Bridge whilst leading the Junior TT. Unhurt, he re-mounted only to retire with a broken exhaust three laps

It was no surprise that Joey won TTs on the RVF750, here seen hustling through Braddan Bridge, but he was no less dominant when he had to ride a 'glorified production bike' in 1988. (Phil Masters)

Joey with Steve Hislop and Geoff Johnson after that furious dice with Steve Cull in the 1988 Senior TT. It would be four years before he'd win another. (Phil Masters)

later. 'The fuel cap kept coming off,' he explained afterwards. 'Then, as I tried to pass Cull and Reid at the same time, I went down.'

By this time, despite struggling with the RVF's unusually poor handling and carburation during practice, Joey had his customary Formula One win in the bag, by over a minute from Geoff Johnson. 'Joey's in a class of his own,' admitted Johnson, 'so whoever finished second is as good as a winner.'

Riding his Formula One bike in the Senior TT, Joey found the RVF's handling problems had returned, and lost three minutes replacing a steering damper bolt. At the finish he lay fourth, over two minutes behind winner Roger Burnett. 'I could have gone better on my 250,'

he complained. 'I'd prepared my 500 the day before but was persuaded to run my F1 bike. It was my decision, and it was wrong. It's got to be the 500 for Senior TTs here.'

Perhaps 1986 was fated to be one of those sorts of year. A season which had begun so brightly with royal recognition had plunged the depths with the deaths of Big Mel, Robinson and Gene McDonnell, not to mention Robert's injuries. Set against all of that, maybe Honda's surprise autumn announcement mattered little, but it still came as a shock. On 1 October at a swanky hotel just off London's Whitehall, Roger Etcel announced that the Honda Britain team was no more. Was Joey Dunlop, MBE, four times World Champion, now unemployed?

Captain Fearless

'He had no fear in him. Even when he was steel erecting, he could walk across a four-inch beam, 100 feet up in the air, without even thinking about it.'

Sammy Graham

In road racing, bloody death is rarely more than a tyre's breadth away, and Joey Dunlop used to get scared just like everybody else. 'Och, you do,' he once told me. 'I have close shaves nearly every time I race, you've just got to keep them to a minimum. Ten minutes later you've forgotten about it.' He went on to describe riding along the Sulby Straight, then a

Clearly chuffed with another F1 win in 1986, Joey is flanked (right to left) by Dave Sleat, Davy Wood and Dunlop tyre boffin Steve Male. (Don Morley)

Opposite: Joey on the RC30 at Parliament Square in 1988, on the way to a remarkable sixth successive Formula One TT win. (Don Morley)

One of the most exquisite racing motorcycles ever created, Honda's RVF750, taking Joey to victory at Assen, 1986. The post-race celebrations were less pretty. (Don Morley)

section of the TT course with bumps violent enough to make your eyes bleed, as 'really dangerous. It was just a question of crossing your fingers and hanging on. There's not a lot you can do about TT safety. It's so quick now, that's the problem.'

Anyone unfamiliar with motorcycle road racing might regard its exponents as courageous in the extreme, if not certifiably mad. But, like many of his opponents, Joey didn't regard himself as especially brave. In fact he clearly disapproved of excessive risk-taking on the track. 'Once you're beat, you're beat,' he would say. 'If you don't accept that, you're going to get hurt. I just ride my own race, and that's that.'

Like most youngsters, the Dunlop kids would take risks for fun. 'We used to go rock jumping, down on the coast,' Jim recalls. 'You had to time it right with a wave, or you were in. Joey was great at egging you on, but he'd always have a go in the end. He was still getting

up to this daft stuff after he'd signed for Honda. As kids we were always clambering up trees and ropes. It wasn't until I started employing people in the roofing business that I knew there was such a thing as a fear of heights.'

On the subject of leaping, if there is a gene for fear, somewhere in the Dunlop family tree it failed to make the jump from one generation to the next. Jim's observation about dread of heights might just as well have come from Joe. And if there was no comprehension of fear, equally there could be little concept of courage. Joey – and Robo and Frank and Jim and Robert and the rest of them – just did what they did. Sure, there was a buzz, and it was somehow related to danger. But winning was also a big part of it. And who has time to think of stuff like this when there's a bike to prepare for a race?

But bravery, bottle, call it what you will – Joey's opponents knew he had it by the crate-

ful. 'He was brave,' asserts former TT star Mick Grant with heavy emphasis, 'and the quick stuff didn't faze him at all. I remember this very fast, blind double bend at Vila Real. I just didn't have the bottle to do it flat. But Joey would howl into it every lap, totally committed. His strength was his confidence in high-speed corners, like Windmill at Dundrod – very, very fast, and blind – he just had total confidence and commitment.'

He was very determined, but very safety conscious too

It was sometimes true on short circuits too. Roger Burnett remembers an early World Superbike round at Hockenheim. 'There were about 13 of us in a snake, going into the Ost Curve … fast and very scary … it was who dared go in quickest. Joey just went round the outside of everyone. So brave.'

Scores of other former opponents say the same. 'If he took the slow bends as well as the fast ones,' suggested Iain Duffus after following Joey at the TT, 'he'd be lapping at 130mph.'

Conor McGinn, a Dubliner who was a sort of honorary Armada man in the mid-Seventies, remembers racing against Joey and constantly asking himself 'How did he do that? Where did he find that bit of tarmac between me and that ditch? He'd be past and gone … he used to see things others didn't. It was genius. Nothing less.'

But that wasn't even the half of it. After following Joey for half a lap during the 1991 Senior TT, Steve Hislop reported that the master's 'line is still spot-on everywhere. He's magic to follow.'

'He was just super smooth,' Hislop explained recently, 'and I'm sure that's why he was always so good in the wet – fast, but he didn't look to be working hard. I remember catching him at Glen Helen once on a 600. He was bit cautious and I followed out of curiosity to see how he was going. Inch perfect. So smooth. I think we had similar lines and style, although he was less hang-off, moved about less than me.'

'He'd got what Mike Hailwood had,' reckons Mick Chatterton, who began racing still earlier than Himself. 'Even when he was going very, very quick, to him he ought to have been even quicker … so smooth and so neat. When he'd come past you in practice you'd try to tuck in,

and often his bike was no quicker – but he'd just pull away. You'd be getting into trouble and sitting up, and he'd still have his chin on the tank.

'He had so much feel for a bike and for conditions. And he was a very intelligent rider. In the wet, he had a great feel for adhesion when there wasn't much. That's why racing in the wet didn't worry him.'

TT regulars became accustomed to Joey's less than impressive practice performances. Sometimes, these were due to machine troubles, but often not. Usually, it was a combination of working bike and rider no harder than needs be, with just a dash of out-foxing thrown in. As he explained at his last TT: 'I know where I can go quick, and I know where the bike's right, so I just go hard on the bits that give me bother.' In other words, he only pushed on the sections he was off the pace, knowing the rest could take care of itself come race day. As a result, his practice lap times were often ordinary.

Nick Jefferies rode against Joey often, and found him 'magic to follow … it seemed so effortless. When you're riding with him he doesn't look fast, he just is. I've ridden with him at the North-West, Dundrod, Scarborough and Macau, as well as the Isle of Man, and he never looked aggressive. His secret was he almost never made mistakes, and I don't think he actually pushed that hard. He had just one TT crash, after all.'

Not that it was always so simple. Bertie Payne still whistles in awe when describing Joey's speed in the wet, which was 'amazing, even early on. I remember him on John Rea's Yamahas at the Killinchy 150, years ago. He was in a class of his own. It would have scared you just to watch. In about 1995 at the Southern 100, it was very wet and misty. I was cleaning the 250, and he wandered by and said I needn't bother – "it's useless today". Then he went out on it and broke the race and lap records, then the same on the 125. Then he took out the 600, just to do "one lap for the fans" – and won. Eventually he told us to get the slicks off the 750 and won on that too. Not bad considering he wasn't even going to go out.'

Although Joey's early years were spent predominantly on short circuits, it was on the hard school of Ireland's unforgiving roads where he first really showed his mettle. As Mick Grant observes, this placed him at a clear – if healthy – disadvantage. 'On English shorts we were learning by crashing a lot,' he admitted. 'Maybe the Irish lads like Joey were learning by staying on. I used to reckon to fall off six times a year. You just couldn't get away with that in Ireland.'

Way back in 1977, Joey himself said much the same: 'English racing is a completely different type of racing. They are all big, broad courses – there's no trees about at all. It's very difficult to adapt to that sort of circuit where you really have to ride hard and not worry about falling off or hitting a tree or something like that. You'd think when you're riding against them that they're completely mad – and I'm just starting to get it into my head that you can afford to fall off in England. That's why they all go so hard.' Later he told Sammy Graham that the difference on the shorts was that you could ride 100 per cent, drift the bike into bends – but 'you couldn't get away with that on the roads'.

Of course it suited Himself for his opponents to think him less able than them at purpose-built tracks like Brands Hatch and Donington Park. If the mood did take him, that gave him an edge. Rob McElnea is by no means alone in suggesting that 'when he put his mind to it, he could be brilliant'.

Wee Robert Dunlop, himself a great short circuit rider, agrees. 'Joey was good on the shorts when he wanted, but I think it was too much like hard work. He was very determined, but very safety conscious too. If he didn't feel as if he was in control, he'd pull in.'

'He was good, better than most people made out', insisted James Whitham. 'I once saw him win at Hockenheim by half a lap – and that's a long lap. He had the best bike but it was still awesome.'

'When it became obvious he was a bit special,' recalls Mick Grant, 'we thought we could beat him on the shorts. Often we could, but I remember going to Aghadowey on the

Opposite: *Joey nails the Harris CBR600 out of Creg-ny-Baa on his way to fourth place – then his best ever on a 600 – in the 1995 Junior TT.* (Phil Masters)

Joey's RC45 gets a push start from Bertie Payne and Sammy Graham at the Ulster in 1995. (Stephen Davison – Pacemaker)

XR69 [1000cc Suzuki] thinking I'd show him the way, and fell off trying to keep up. I think, if he wanted, he could do the shorts. He often had a sort of holiday racer attitude – he'd be quick when he could be bothered – which made him inconsistent. We used to joke that if you lined all the shorts with a brick-effect wallpaper, he'd have been unbeatable.'

If he was smooth and brave, one thing he was not, at least not in the Eighties, was conspicuously fit. Physical training wasn't high on the Dunlop agenda. 'He'd have thrown up at the thought of it,' reckons Grant. 'Once we were at Vila Real, and Nigel Everett [Mick's mechanic] bought me a drink for my birthday. Joey wanders by, asks what's going on, next thing there's another round of brandies, about a third of a pint each. Then another, then another. At about 9.30 I left them to it. Next morning Nigel looked wicked. Said they'd carried on, then gone for a lap of the circuit. Joey was driving but the brandy bottle kept getting tangled in the steering, so they were mostly sideways.

'The car was parked halfway up the hotel steps, and Joey spent the next two days in bed. He was obviously out of it. "I've got you, now," I thought to myself. He got out of bed for practice, qualified, and won the race, the bastard. Then he collapsed and had to be put on a drip.'

Yarns such as that speak volumes about the man's bottomless determination. But unlike most successful sportsmen, he wasn't obviously competitive. His will to win wasn't in your face. No winning instinct shrieked at you, the way it did with Kenny Roberts or Carl Fogarty, men who couldn't bear to lose at anything. Slick Bass prepared bikes for Joey in 1987 and for Fogarty for each of his four World Superbike titles, and is uniquely placed to make the comparison: 'Foggy raced to win, that's all he cared about. But Joey loved racing. He'd have club raced if he had to, and loved that as well. There wasn't an obvious fire in his eyes like with Carl.'

'Och,' laughs Linda of her laid-back spouse, 'he could play darts and not be bothered who won.' But on two wheels, when it mattered, winning was the stuff Joey enjoyed most. 'He liked it,' insists Mick Grant, a man who should know. 'I've seen that glint in his eye on the rostrum. He enjoyed it. He liked the winning.'

He also liked to prove doubters wrong, particularly later in his career when he wasn't considered so dominant. 'David [Jefferies] and Phillip [McCallen] have both said that when Joey got a notion to win, no-one could touch him,' reckons Sammy Graham, 'but how did you give him the notion? We used to joke about

Opposite: *Cranking through the Gooseneck on the way to that final, fairy-tale 2000 Formula One win.* (Phil Masters)

In appalling conditions Joey foxed his way to victory in the 1998 Lightweight TT, arguably the most courageous ride of his career. (Phil Masters)

riling him up to win races – maybe tickling him between the legs with a nettle. Before one race in '95, which looked like being wet, one opponent was saying he thought that Brian Reid would be a threat, but Joey wouldn't be. Joey heard, and went out and murdered them, in the wet. Last year [1999] at the Ulster, David Jefferies made the same mistake, and Joey decided to put him in his place. He always raced fairly hard but it took something extra to put him in the right frame of mind to win – some comment, or something in the paper.'

Plenty of racers have had a point to prove. Plenty are driven by the same need to succeed without even winning one TT. What, other than

sheer longevity, lifted Joey above the herd?

Mechanical empathy was certainly one attribute. 'Joey was always easy on an engine,' Sammy Graham explained. 'He didn't over-rev them, and he was easy on the gearbox.'

To Davy Wood, Joey 'nurtured bikes around the Isle of Man. He had an affinity with them … knew what he had to do to make them last'. That affinity surely began when, as a child, he watched Willie ply his trade in the shadow of the windmill on Bravallen Road.

Curly Scott puts it more succinctly: 'He had the most sensitive backside of any rider who ever lived.'

Charlie Williams, nine times a TT winner

Mr and Mrs Joey Dunlop, relaxing in the bar. (Joey Dunlop Family Collection)

it. And if he had any doubt, Jackie [Graham] was the man he'd ask about technical things. He thought Jackie was a very intelligent man. And he had a lot of faith in Robert's expertise with the 125.'

Joey's routines and habits were as idiosyncratic as the man, and showed the same single-mindedness. Long before the word was fashionable, Joey was already the most focused of sportsmen. 'He'd often work right through the night,' grins Liam. 'That way he wouldn't get any interruptions and he could sleep through the day and avoid people then too.'

Bertie Payne, Joey's 250 sponsor throughout the Nineties, remembers that 'he had his own wee ways of doing things. If he took it into his head that one person could do something, even if there were 50 stood around and ready, it had to be that one. And nobody ever contradicted him in any shape or form.'

His apparent eccentricity sometimes had a basis, as when a Honda mechanic dropped Joey's filler cap inside the fairing during a pit-stop. 'We had to pick the bike up and sort of shake it out,' recalls Ernie Coates. 'After that he'd have to have his own man doing the fuel, usually me. He was like that with every job – not that he'd give you much notice. He'd usually ask me if I could do the fuel five minutes before the race. Anyway, I haven't seen him race since I was signalling, and even then I only saw him at the Gooseneck.

'But he wouldn't trust just anyone to do the signalling. He'd have me, John Rae, Curly. And my son Mark used to do it at the 13th, with Norman Dunne's son. He was only 11 or 12 at the time, but Joey trusted him.'

Roger Marshall, who came so agonisingly close to denying Joey the world Formula One crown in 1984, was taken aback by Joey's performance at the 2000 TT. 'We were almost the same age, so I was shocked when he did the treble. When you think how hard I used to train, and never won a TT – it just shows how great Joey was to win at that age. He was just such a natural, had such phenomenal natural ability. But he had an aggressive side to him too. Joey may have been quiet but he was no pushover.'

and now a Radio TT pundit, describes Joey as 'one of the most incredible TT riders there's ever been, but it's hard to say exactly why. Obviously he had superb circuit knowledge, and he was very good at setting bikes up. But what perplexed me was where he found the motivation and will to keep taking the obvious risks. Obviously he still loved riding there – and, come to think of it, I can understand that.'

Unlike practically every other top rider of the modern era, Joey also got as much satisfaction from working on his race bikes as from riding them. As time passed, Joey's chief mechanic became Joey himself, a role he insisted on playing for all but the most exotic factory bikes. 'Every new bike,' Andy Inglis recalls, 'Joey had to pull it down – take it totally to pieces – before he'd ride it.'

Liam Beckett, better known as Robert's mechanic but also a former associate of Joey, agrees: 'He'd never take anything at face value. Honda could send him a new go-faster part like a special carburettor, but he'd have to strip it and understand how it worked before he'd use

On the Slide?

*'Soichiro Honda had said that if you're winning the TT, you're selling motorbikes, and they believed this.
That's partly why Joey was so important to them.'*

TT winner Nick Jefferies

If there was any possibility at Chiswick that Honda might pull out of Formula One, no such notion existed back at headquarters in Japan. Scarcely had the ink dried on the newspaper announcements of Honda Britain's shock withdrawal from domestic racing in October 1986, than Honda Japan forced a rethink. 'I was still under contract to HRC,' remembers Barry Symmons. 'They made it very clear to Honda Britain that if they didn't run a Formula One team, there would be no Grand Prix team either.'

Reminded emphatically of Soichiro Honda's absolute commitment to the TT – and thus to Joey – Power Road quickly adopted Plan B for British and World Formula Racing. With Symmons concentrating on Grand Prix, Peter McNab was drafted in as team manager. For Joey's major meetings, Nick Goodison, back from Suzuki as senior mechanic, worked alongside a young Slick Bass. Joey's main bike for the campaign, still in Rothmans livery, was an American Superbike-spec V-four.

By way of a Honda 'thank you present', Joey was also allowed to contest the 500cc British Grand Prix that year. (Joey's only Grand Prix points had come two years before at Silverstone, when he placed 10th in the 250cc class.) 'He blew the minds of the Japanese,' reckons Nick Jefferies. 'They couldn't weigh him up, but worshipped him all the same. But if there was a decline, it began with Honda's withdrawal from top-flight racing, rather than with anything Joey ever did.'

'The Superbike thing we had that year didn't

There were no smiles when America's Fred Merkel (left) punted Joey off at Assen in 1987. World Superbike 'inventor' Steve McLauchlin grins in the background. (Honda Europe)

handle,' recalls Goodison. 'But with Barry more concerned with Wayne [Gardner] and Roger [Burnett], we were left to our own devices. So our problems were falling on deaf ears until the TT. Anyway, Barry couldn't possibly believe that Honda had produced a duff bike. It wasn't slow, but as a package it wasn't a patch on the RVF.

'Then Joey went and blitzed the F1 race. Barry sidled up at the finish and said, "is that the bike that doesn't handle?" It didn't help our cause for the rest of the year, but Joey was never happy with the bike.'

But Joey who? 'Joey Michelin' ran the ads, of the man who'd defected from Dunlop tyres to win the Formula One TT yet again. 'Make sure it's a Michelin – Yer Man did.' The bike press, meanwhile, was busy predicting that 'the 120mph lap is on'. At less than 100mph, Joey's next win was his second slowest ever, but perhaps his greatest. 'Dunlop rains Supreme' sang the papers, after Joey splashed through the Manx monsoon in a Senior TT postponed to Saturday. Riding a 500 triple that he had prepared himself, he won by almost a minute from Geoff Johnson's 1000cc Yamaha.

Mick Grant was Suzuki team manager, in charge of Phil 'Mez' Mellor, who led until he slid off at the Nook. 'On the start line, I knew we had it,' Grant recalls, 'and told Mez so. We were on the right tyres and Joey was on the wrong ones, yet he still won. Magnificent.'

Bob McMillan got things more happily wrong. 'I was amazed when Joey asked my advice about what he should ride, but said the 500 if it's dry, the four-stroke if it's wet. He did the complete opposite of what I'd said – and won the race.'

Joey described the four-lap race as graphically as he can ever have done. It was 'raceable on the first lap but after that, dreadful … dangerous. On the first lap I aquaplaned all the way down Bray Hill, then had a big moment on new tar at Black Hut. The bike went four times from lock to lock trying to spit me over the top … I thought I was down but stayed on … on the last lap I caught a dozen backmarkers in the mist. You couldn't see Creg-ny-Baa until you were on it. All the people who stayed on to watch deserved a medal.'

So Joey was the same as ever, but unfortunately the Formula One World Championship was not. Indeed it was so different that Virginio Ferrari was able to wrest the title without once racing on public roads. Events conspired to increase the short-circuit bias when Imatra failed to meet safety standards, and Vila Real was shelved as a result – in a roundabout way – of a Portuguese general election.

The series began well enough with third at Misano, behind Paul Iddon's Suzuki and Fred Merkel's Honda. Two weeks later the circus was at the Hungaroring, memorably described by Himself as 'just like Aghadowey'. Maybe it was, because the Londonderry short circuit hadn't always been kind to Joey either. On a notoriously 'front-endy' track that palpably did not suit his style, he suffered his first practice crash in four seasons. In the race, the Bimotas of Ferrari and Tardozzi took full advantage as a battered Joey struggled to eighth and the Suzukis of Iddon and Marshall both crashed out.

No matter. The Island was next and a fifth

Slick Bass (kneeling) and Nick Goodison (holding helmet) help Joey prepare to ride a VFR-based racer at Donington Park in 1987 watched by Roger Etcel, Honda's promotions boss. (Phil Masters)

Like Foggy a decade later, Joey adored Assen's fast, flowing curves, although 1988 proved a deeply disappointing Dutch TT. (Don Morley)

Formula One win on the trot hoisted him to the top of the standings. Then it all went wrong at Assen. Flying Fred Merkel collected his Honda buddy hurtling into the chicane, leaving Joey venting his frustration with a two-fingered salute to the American. Ferrari, the winner, now led Joey by two points – but with Dundrod to come.

Any hopes the Italian may have had of taking points from Ulster evaporated when he toured the circuit, pronounced it 'too dangerous' and hopped on the next plane home. But Irish relief was cut short in the most brutal way. In appallingly wet conditions, many riders pressed for the race not to start at all. Scarcely had it begun when Germany's Klaus Klein hit standing water and slid off, suffering fatal injuries. The meeting was abandoned.

Joey then trudged out to Japan with little prospect of points in a race usually dominated by home riders. In the event Australia's Kevin Magee and a young Michael Doohan placed first and third, with Anders Andersson the sole European scorer in seventh. The Swede aside, it was a desperate day for Europe. Joey placed 12th, with Ferrari failing to finish when he clipped Joey's rear wheel and slid off. Marshall also crashed out, with Tardozzi and Iddon retiring. In championship terms, it was as meaningless as it was expensive.

A win at Hockenheim to Joey's stubborn fourth took Ferrari a further seven points clear

Steve Ryder quizzes a smart-looking Joey on letting the title go again in 1988, to a fresh-faced Carl Fogarty. (Don Morley)

of the champion, leaving everything down to Donington Park. Taking ten points out of a rider as able and experienced as the 34-year-old Italian on a 'pure' short circuit was always going to be tough. Joey didn't help his cause by starting poorly on the same factory Honda that had won the Bol d'Or seven days earlier. In other circumstances, third place ahead of Fred Merkel might have been a result, but with Ferrari cruising into seventh, the title was gone. Joey may still have been King of the Roads, but he was no longer King of the World.

1988

Honda's Bob McMillan was the man upstairs responsible for ensuring that Honda Britain's much reduced 1988 race effort got onto the road. He had first met Joey in 1984 when charged with looking after him at the annual *Motor Cycle News* Awards. After a few glasses of Dutch courage in the pub next door, Joey had picked up the 'Man of the Year' gong. 'We carried on drinking afterwards,' remembers McMillan of his first night of works swallowing. 'It was the first time in years I'd actually been physically sick.'

He says of the hastily assembled Shell Gemini race effort: 'It was a bit chaotic. But thank God for Joey. You can't trust everyone in racing, but you could trust Joey. He'd rather buy something himself than bother you with it. True, sometimes on the Isle of Man I'd get both barrels – him and Linda both telling me the problems he was having with the bikes. But you could depend on him.' From now on Honda would provide only the bikes and parts, with running costs met from sponsorship, prize and appearance money.

With the race effort focused entirely on Ballymoney, mechanics like Sammy Graham were glad to be more actively back on board, although there was a limit to what any wrencher could do. 'If something needed doing, Joey's first instinct,' explained Sammy, 'was to do it himself, even if there was a mechanic standing around doing nothing. So the smaller races I didn't go to – just the big meetings where he had a lot of bikes.'

The new arrangement also brought Nick Goodison a year to remember, not only as chief mechanic but as a member of the Dunlop household on Garryduff Road. It began with a call from Davy Wood, who 'asked if I'd be interested in working for Joey with the new

RC30. It took a fair while to get the season up and running. We were only just in time for the first race. But what a year ... you like to think you can drink as well as the next bloke, but – Christ! – some of those sessions ...'

Joey's crew, nicknamed 'The Clampitts' in certain quarters, were sometimes dismissed as a particularly hard-drinking joke. But there was a lot more to them than that. 'His entourage was unbelievable,' chuckles Nick Goodison, still impressed by the motivational impact his man had. 'They'd go to any lengths – any lengths at all – to help. And they could do things. They had lathes, welding kit, spray booths, you name it. They had everything covered and could get any job done, and do it well.

'Whatever Joey said, went, but others would chip in things that he would take on board. And

A roll-call of sponsors, from the early Eighties until the end. (Gavan Caldwell – Pacemaker)

the hours they used to put in for him! They were unbelievable friendships. But unless you knew Joey you wouldn't know he was grateful. He was as secretive about that as everything else. You'd get your thanks on the quiet. I was on a good wage, but they wouldn't let me spend a penny, all year. I couldn't even buy a drink. And Linda's Irish breakfasts – wow! – every day.

'But it was strange. After those glorious Rothmans Honda years, here I was working in Joey's garage on nothing special – a bike like anyone could buy. It was like club racing again, a bit of a culture shock. There'd be kittens all over the workshop, and kids playing with racing pistons in the rain. It was funny in a way, but I don't think Joey gave of his best that year. To my mind he was spending too much time working on the bikes. There was hardly any organisation. Everything was last minute.

'Sure, we had a good TT. But you could take Joey there on a BSA Bantam and he'd still do the business.'

There was no BSA Bantam, although press reports suggested Joey was 'miffed' at 'having to make do with a race-kitted RC30'. Joey allegedly warned Honda that he wouldn't be riding for them in 1989 'unless they come up with a good explanation'. If true, he had little reason to be bothered, for the 'good TT' described by Goodison was Joey's second triple win: Formula One, Junior, Senior.

A race week that began with new race and lap records as Joey stormed to his habitual Formula One win also gave notice of a threat on the horizon. The danger to Joey came not from a lack of machinery, but from the man even Joey was calling 'the new pretender'. That same Steve Hislop who'd gawped from the grassy bank at the 11th Milestone in 1983 was now Joey's team-mate. It was Joey's week, to be sure, but Hislop spent much of race week yapping at his heels.

In the Senior it was Joey's compatriot Steve Cull who did the pushing. Riding the same 500cc two-stroke used by Joey the previous year, Cull had already broken outright records at Cookstown and Tandragee. Joey can't have been surprised, since he'd predicted in May that any of the Honda triples ridden by Cull,

Laycock or Reid could be lapping at record pace. In a ferocious tussle, Joey and Cull both broke the old lap record on lap two, and lay level on corrected time after lap three. Then Cull holed an expansion pipe, eventually setting fire to the bike. He pulled in on the drop to Brandish and stood impotently by as the fastest bike in TT history burned out.

At the finish, with Hislop 50 seconds behind, Joey's main problem was a sore neck. Race preparation had been typically hurried. The bike had been run in at Jurby, at night, using car headlights to navigate. Usually this was Davy Wood's job, and his scariest and least favourite of the year. On the way to scrutineering the next morning, a box of spares fell on the bike in the van, breaking Joey's only tall screen. Denied its protection, he finished the 226-mile race covered in dead flies and with aching neck muscles.

Still, he could have had worse luck in claiming TT win number 13. Or maybe he did: after customary victory celebrations, Joey woke in the middle of the night to find he was out of smokes. He got out of bed and jumped into the car, only to bump into a copper keen enough to notice a defective rear light in the small hours. Police described Joey as 'very quiet, co-operative and steady on his feet', but breathalysed him all the same. He was banned from driving for 18 months and fined £200.

Joey was desperate to get back his Formula One world crown. Sitting out the opening round in Sugo, Japan, cost him nothing. Of the series contenders, only Anders Andersson made the trip, crashing out of tenth place. With a successful TT behind him, Joey caught the ferry to Holland looking good. But yet again Assen proved a disaster. Joey started poorly and struggled with a sick engine to place eighth, leaving Honda-mounted winner Burnett topping the championship standings. In his first overseas race, young Carl Fogarty finished ninth.

For once Vila Real failed to frazzle the racers. It was a wet shambles instead. Joey led after six laps, only for a downpour to halt the race. Fogarty led the re-start, retired with water in the ignition, then watched as darkness forced

You could give Joey a Bantam and he'd still do the business

Opposite: *North-West 200, 1996: Bertie Payne and Joey ponder over the BitMac 250 Honda.* (Alastair McCook)

the re-start to be abandoned after 10 laps – 23 miles short of the FIM's minimum distance. As a result, only half points could be awarded. Burnett, absent on Superbike duty in Austria, retained the championship lead.

In Finland Joey was in a comfortable second place when his RC30 seized entering the last corner. Luckily he was able to coast over the line with the loss of only one place, with Fogarty relegated to fourth by an additional fuel stop. With a 14-point lead and the Ulster Grand Prix ahead, surely it was in the bag?

Despite a damp track, Joey chose slick tyres at Dundrod. It was a mistake. Pitting for inter-mediate rubber dropped him way down the field and he had to fight hard even to claw his way back to seventh. Despite a poor qualifying performance, Fogarty romped through the pack to win by an impressive 16 seconds from Hislop, both on Hondas.

Even worse was to come in Sicily, where Joey clipped a kerb and crashed going 'too fast, too soon' on the unfamiliar Pergusa circuit. Too battered to tackle the final qualifying sessions, Joey heaved his injured arm onto the handle-bars for the race, only to discover his engine to be in even worse shape than himself: a valve spring had broken. He could only watch in frus-tration as Fogarty saw off local Bimota man Gianluca Galasso to take maximum points. With just Donington Park to come three weeks later, Foggy led by 14.5 points.

In a field peppered with short-circuit special-ists, and still handicapped by his injured arm, Joey would have stood little chance even had Fogarty not finished. In the event the future World Superbike hero rode with impressive calm to claim fifth spot, with Joey a distant 11th. The title went to Blackburn, by 20.5 points.

'I'm not too sick about it', Joey claimed afterwards. 'I've had a good TT and that's my main thing.' Little can he have known that it would be fully 20 months before he scored another World Championship point.

1989

It was especially ironic that in the year in which the World Formula One Championship came

I'm not too sick – I've had a good TT and that's my main thing

closer to its true road race roots, the finest exponent of road racing should sit out the series through injury. More ironic yet, those injuries were sustained at Brands Hatch – supposedly a far safer circuit than most on which Joey rode.

The accident happened on 24 March – Good Friday – during the Eurolantic match race series. On the tenth lap of the third match race, going into Paddock Bend, Belgium's Stephane Mertens clipped Joey's rear wheel and sent him cartwheeling into the tyre barrier. James Whitham was right behind the incident, and shakes his head in recollection: 'It looked a bad one.' Spectators remember Joey 'buried under a tyre wall … then on the stretcher, arms crossed on his chest … it looked serious … the worst.'

For what it's worth, Roger Burnett won the re-started race and Britain beat a contrived 'Rest of the World' squad by a crushing 900–484. Joey, meanwhile, languished in the medical centre. By an ironic coincidence, in the next cubicle was team-mate Steve Hislop who'd slid off in another race and got an eyeful of grit. 'I felt really sorry for the poor wee sod, but gutted too – bang goes our head-to-head at the TT.'

Joey's injuries were serious but not life-threatening. At St Mary's Hospital, just down the road in Sidcup, doctors operated on his smashed right wrist. Later his broken left thigh was pinned, then pinned again when the first pin proved to be too short. But he wasn't happy. Bob McMillan describes the day Honda press man Graham Sanderson went to see Joey in hospital. 'He was so brassed off with the way they were treating him he was even talking of getting someone to load him into a van and drive him home. So we had him flown to Belfast in an air ambulance. Linda was in hospital at the same time having Joanne.'

Back in civilisation, Joey's wrist was re-set – correctly, this time – and he could finally begin his recuperation. In Honda's 30th anniversary TT year he was entered for no less than six races. Come late May, he had been passed fit to ride in Ireland, but the ACU had other ideas. TT Press Officer Peter Kneale, who

Joey shares the rostrum with Virginio Ferrari, the man who took his World Formula One title, during 1987. (Clifford McLean)

commentated on every one of Joey's TT rides, remembers seeing him 'swinging past the press office on crutches, on his way to being knocked back' by the medical officer. Evidently the leg was strong enough – or so Joey reckoned – but not the crucial right wrist.

If 1989 was Joey's most disappointing TT – the only one he would miss in 25 years – it was also the event that established beyond any doubt the affection in which he was held by race fans. Bob McMillan recalls getting special permission to take him for a lap of honour on the back of a CBR1000 after the Senior. 'All the crowds were waving and clapping, almost invading the track. But it was a struggle for him, hanging on with his good arm and waving with the bad one. "Never again" he said when he got off.'

A couple of days earlier, at the Villa Marina Awards Presentation, Joey got an even more rapturous reception. In front of several thou-

sand gleeful witnesses, McMillan publicly promised Joey race bikes for as long as he wanted them. 'I wanted to help him,' he explained. 'I had such feelings for the lad if he did decide to come back, which I thought would have been good for Honda as well as for Joey. In the same way I'll never understand why Honda didn't support Hailwood when he came back – surely one of the worst racing decisions Honda ever made.'

Joey was 37 years old and badly knocked about. It might have been a good time to consider retirement. If he did so, this didn't show. Indeed the bike press soon promised he'd be 'back next year to try to better Hailwood's record of 14 TT wins'. Meanwhile Carl Fogarty clinched his second Formula One title for Honda at Dundrod on 12 August, by eight points from team-mate Steve Hislop. The highest-placed Dunlop was Robert, in third. For a while he'd be carrying the family flag.

Some Dotage

'He'd be lapped at places like Kirkistown. People were saying he was finished, he should retire.'

Sammy Graham, of Joey's come-back year

On the road to recovery, Joey battles Robert at the North-West 200 in 1990. 'Joey and I never raced for money' said the wee brother. (Clifford McLean – Pacemaker)

'That was a turning point in his life,' reckons Robert Dunlop of Joey's Brands Hatch crash. 'Before, I think he thought he couldn't be beat. But after that he was a long time on the mend and lost his drive, got a bit demoralised, and got into a rut. If you look at

his [TT] wins, most were by being canny or after other riders had problems. And on the big bikes, because he wasn't looking after himself, he was bound to lose out to McCallen on the physical parts of the TT lap.

As would later be the case with the question

of retirement, Joey was sometimes prepared to seek quiet advice. Nick Jefferies, for many years a Honda team-mate, remembers such an instance in Macau, the year after the Brands crash. 'We had a long chat about coming back from injury, because I'd been hurt at the TT that year. Joey was saying it was taking him a long, long time to get the confidence back, and for him that was what racing was all about.'

If Joey was inspiring whilst winning races, he was no less so as a comparatively mediocre mid-field rider. Fans and opponents alike were impressed by the way he got stuck in, racing purely for the fun of it. But slowly he got back on the pace. His first win came on 6 July 1991, at Skerries on Andy McMenemy's 125.

A month later he was back at his beloved Dundrod. Sammy Graham remembers it well. 'The only race where he really punched the air crossing the finish line was at the Ulster when he beat Robert on the Norton. It was his first big win after the accident. He said himself it was the only time he really celebrated. He was back.'

Joey's principal private sponsors, from this time until the end of his career, would be Andy McMenemy with the 125, Bertie Payne with the 250 and, from 1991, John Harris with the CBR600 Supersport machine. The yen for a 600 came out of the blue, as Davy Wood explained: 'It was a big surprise when Joey expressed interest in a CBR, because he'd always distrusted road tyres. But [Castrol Honda race boss] Neil Tuxworth introduced us to John Harris, and we had nine great years with him.'

Like most Irish road race fans, Bertie Payne had known Joey to nod to for years. 'I well mind him in the paddock at Kirkistown,' he remembers of the early days, 'welding away at a Yamaha frame, getting up, kicking it, and the whole thing falling to bits. But he got it done eventually. We got to know each other in 1988 when I lent him a bike for a Children In Need event at the Forum Hotel.' In February 1989 at the Antrim Show, they shook hands on the deal which would last out Joey's career.

'And what main jet do you have in there?' Joey and Robert at the North-West 200. (Clifford McLean – Pacemaker)

In Joey's Bar in 1992 Ferodo presented Himself with a trophy commemorating his record-equalling 14th TT win. (Clifford McLean)

Joey posing at Buckingham Palace with the sublime Honda VFR750 road bike which his racing experience had helped develop. (Honda Europe)

Opposite: On the RS250 at the North-West in 1994. In later years Joey regarded the circuit's ultra-long straights as no true test of a rider. (Clifford McLean – Pacemaker)

Joey draws for inspiration at Carrowdore in 1993. 'I hate these things' he said, and then gave up. (Stephen Davison – Pacemaker)

1990

'Dunlop Roars to Same Day Treble.' The headline had a wonderfully familiar ring, but the Dunlop in question was Robert, and the triple was at the North-West 200. Joey placed fourth on the 750, and the same on the 125.

On the global stage, this was the year that Formula One became merely the FIM Cup, losing true World Championship status. For Joey, not yet back to full form or fitness, the distinction was academic. Only Honda Britain contested every round, and the only real opposition to Fogarty was Norton.

After sitting out the opening round at Sugo, and struggling to a weary eighth place at the TT, Joey performed creditably well. Third at Vila Real, fifth at Kouvola, Finland, then on 11 August that fairy-tale win at Dundrod. His first international win since 1988 had been no fluke. He'd emerged from a stirring dice with Robert with a new lap record at almost 123mph. 'Just like the good old days,' he grinned on the rostrum. Fogarty took the Formula One title once more, but Joey placed second, five points clear of Robert.

In the smaller classes, Joey was already competitive even in the long TT races, as he showed whilst tussling with Ian Newton for second place in the 1990 Ultra-Lightweight event. But backing for the middle-aged has-been wasn't so easy to get. Financially, these were his leanest years. For 1991 the 'Team Dunlop' bikes were mainly white and strangely lacking in sponsors' stickers.

1991

The TT was ignominious. Honda brought in two exotic RVF 750s – the very machine Joey had helped develop – but not for Himself to ride. Hislop and Fogarty, the new TT heroes, would ride them instead. Whilst they dismantled the outright lap record on their factory projectiles, Joey just got on with business – and came within an ace of equalling Mike Hailwood's record of 14 TT wins.

The event, predictably, was the 125cc Ultra-Lightweight race. But for a broken fuel

Willie Dunlop, Joey's dad, had 'a big influence on him,' according to Linda Dunlop. (Stephen Davison – Pacemaker)

breather pipe – and wee Robert's determination – he might have turned the early lead into victory. 'I couldn't see with all the petrol on the inside of the screen,' he explained afterwards. 'I had to stick my head over it, and you'll never win on one of these if you do that.'

In Friday's Senior, with Fogarty contesting Superbikes elsewhere, Joey finally raced again on a real RVF. It was a sentimental reunion. On the final lap, Hislop caught Joey as they entered Ramsey, and the duo rode in formation across the Mountain before crossing the

finish line side-by-side. As the RVF 'pulled the arms out of' him, Joey recorded his fastest-ever TT lap: 121.51mph, finishing second.

1992

Maybe, with his 40th birthday approaching, he was getting back to the Joey of old? Six wins at the Southern 100, followed by a Superbike double at Dundrod, certainly suggested as much. The 1992 Formula One TT was just like the good old days, although not in an ideal way. Just as in 1980, he held the fuel tank on with his knees when a bracket broke at Quarter Bridge. Overall in the larger classes, rising stars McCallen and Hislop shared the spoils.

Hailwood's record had by now become something of a psychological barrier, for onlookers as for Joey himself. If he was to equal it, the 125cc class was again the key. Joey had prepared hard, even crash-dieting to achieve something closer to Robert's power-to-weight ratio. So he was dispirited that practice had not gone well. Joey stood eighth on the leaderboard on the McMenemy Honda, almost three mph down on leader Robert. 'Nothing seemed to go right,' he shrugged. 'We did four laps and never finished one without a problem. We worked on the bike until 1.30 in the morning, put in a new ignition from Ernie Coates, then found one of the engine mountings had broken. We couldn't get a replacement at that time of day, so used one that Robert had thrown out.'

Against all reasonable expectations 'the bike ran right for the first time this year' and everything came good on the day. In a ferocious race fought at record speed, a mere one fifth of a second separated the brothers at their pit stop, but Joey turned the tables to beat Robert by 8.4 seconds. In the process he took over 23 seconds off his brother's lap record. After the garlanding Joey acknowledged that he'd 'never been classed as a 125 rider but it was good to go out there and beat my brother Robert after he had won the race for the previous three years. I even broke the lap record to prove it was no fluke. It's the first time I've raced hard here for years, but it's all worked out well.' Mixed with the obvious delight, something touching was there to be seen as well. The Man was clearly awed to be sitting on the same pedestal as Mike Hailwood.

'Maybe he'll pack up now and give us all a chance,' Robert responded with more wryness than conviction. Not if the fans had anything to do with it. Three thousand of Joey's army packed into the Villa Marina prizegiving to applaud their man. 'It was frightening,' said their humble hero, 'you'd have thought I'd done a 130mph lap. All those people down there. And the noise. I felt safer going down Bray Hill.' In a small postscript, Norton's Senior victory also brought Barry Symmons his own 14th TT win as a team manager.

1993

This was a full-on year for Joey. Not only was he made a Freeman of Ballymoney – an honour that clearly gave him great pride – but he seemed to be taking his racing more seriously too. A full Irish season was planned, on 125 and 250, 600 and 750cc machines. And nothing belied Joey's age more than winning the normally youthful, and always keenly-fought, Regal 600 Series on John Harris' CBR600.

In the TT it was business as usual, with a win in the Ultra-Lightweight division. Again, practice week went poorly, with several sessions washed out, leaving him sixth in the standings.

Joey tips the RC45 into Ramsey Hairpin on the way to winning the 1995 Senior race. For all its TT success, the big Honda was always a bit of a handful on The Island. (Don Morley)

By the mid-Nineties Joey was beginning
to feel his age – something had to give.
(Gavan Caldwell – Pacemaker)

Opposite: *Joey swings John Harris's
CBR600 round Ginger Hall, on the way
to an ill-handling ninth place in the 1992
Supersport 600 TT.* (Phil Masters)

Not 21 today, but winning his 21st TT
with a 125–250 double in 1996.
(Double Red)

And yet again, Robert was second, this time
only 12 seconds behind, despite riding in pain
from a practice crash at Waterworks on Friday
evening – right in front of his brother.

The win was Joey's 15th, an all-time record.
As he made his way to the rostrum he was
predictably mobbed by delirious well-wishers
chanting 'We love Joey'. He responded with the
usual shy smile, and nod of humility to the TT
giants whose feats he'd surpassed. 'The reception I got on the last lap was incredible,' he
choked, 'way greater than last year when I
equalled the record. I reckon every marshal on
the course must have been waving. In the entire
race, apart from the pit stop, I only lifted my
head above the screen once – to get a signal
from John Rea at Windy Corner on the last
lap.'

A busy year was rounded off when Joey
competed in the Classic Manx Grand Prix – his
first, as a novice. He retired Terry Teece's
Aermacchi at the foot of Bray Hill on lap two,
having been flat-out for almost all of the previous 38 miles. Perhaps anything else would have
been one fairy-tale too far. A year later he
placed third on the same hard-pressed
machine, rendered rather more Joey-proof in
the intervening 12 months.

1994

In an otherwise bleak TT, and having been
narrowly out-gunned at the North-West 200,
practice week went ominously well for Joey.
Fourth on the 125 leaderboard, and third in
both the Junior and F1/Senior were unimag-
ined riches compared with most recent years.

Then, in Mad Sunday's re-run Formula One
TT, it began to go wrong. 'I was just out of
Barregarrow when I saw the van … but had
time to swerve past,' said Joey of his crazy
encounter with an errant Manx Highways lorry.
A lap later at the Highlander he encountered a
dog running around on the track. Then, after
finishing third behind Hislop and McCallen, he
learns that Robert is gravely injured in Nobles
Hospital. Robert's rear wheel had collapsed at
Ballaugh, hurling him into a stone cottage wall.

'Robert and me are very close and it was

tough to race on knowing he was ill,' confessed Joey four days later. By this time, remarkably, he was another two TT wins to the good. Victory in the Ultra-Lightweight race had been comparatively straightforward, by 61 seconds from Dennis McCullough. 'I won this one for him' he said emotionally of his injured brother Robert after the race. 'I just wish wee Robert had been out there racing with me.'

The win meant that a Dunlop had won every Ultra-Lightweight TT since the class was reintroduced in 1989 – three apiece to Robert and Joey. Both brothers could claim some credit for them all. 'One year a friend got a 125 Honda, new,' explains Robert. 'I was so jealous, but Joey bought me one for the next season, after he'd won his first F1 title. It was his wee toy. He

loved tinkering with it, adding his own touch. He put on mechanical anti-dive off his F1 bike. I went out and won my first road race – Temple 100 – on that 125. After that I won pretty much everything. Eventually it turned full circle. By around 1988 he thought I could set up a 125 better than anyone else.'

The 250cc win had owed more to good fortune. Joey stalled his bike on the line, but after that the luck ran his way. For the second year running McCallen ran out of fuel whilst leading, leaving Joey to win by 25.6 seconds from Brian Reid, battling braking problems on his Yamaha. 'My only problem,' explained Joey after, 'was the right footpeg hanging off. My foot kept slipping off, especially when I changed direction. I had to rest my boot on the exhaust.'

Joey hurries out of the Braddan Bridge S-bend on the way to seventh place in the Supersport 600 TT, 1994. (Phil Masters)

Opposite: TT 1995: as ever, Davy Wood has the tab on, but Joey would quit smoking two months later. (Phil Masters)

'Jammy sod,' grinned Ian Lougher: 'When that footrest bolt fell out, anyone else would have lost the rest, but not Joey.'

1995

On the face of it 1995 was little more remarkable than '94, for Joey won yet another two TTs. Yet as well as a full season of Irish meetings, Joey was racing in what would become the 'Pure Roads' series. It was a heavy schedule for any rider, let alone one aged 43, and would prove a landmark in the man's approach to himself, and to his racing.

Sammy Graham remembers it well: 'He stopped smoking, which helped a lot, and started training. He'd come up here to use my weights, and it transformed him. He was tired after a TT, sure, but as sound as anyone else.'

Linda would 'see him lighting a cigarette and saying "I hate these things", but carrying on. He had a sickness every morning when he smoked and was proud of himself for stopping. He hated seeing photos of himself with a cigarette in his mouth, which all the papers seemed to use.'

Robert got a daily dose of the other – funny – side: 'When he got this keep fit notion into his head, he'd be working for Jim steel erecting and whenever he dropped things, he'd sprint down and up again, keeping fit. Of course all Jim saw was the time it cost on the job. There were plenty of people around who could have thrown whatever it was back up.'

Maybe there was no way that, at the age of 43, Joey could have won one of the TT's big classes without getting back into shape. It was all very well quitting the tabs and running up and down ladders, but what of the RC45? In 1994, Joey later admitted, their handling problems were such that 'at the start of practice we were ready to go home'.

Steve Hislop remembers that year 'when the RC45 was so wild and out of control. I was only riding that one bike, but Joey and Phillip had their 125s and 250s as well, so I was trying to set up the 750 for all of us. I remember I got two sets of forks re-valved by Ron Williams, and Joey borrowed my spare set. In fact I think he used them for the rest of the year.'

In 1995 Nick Jefferies recalls an equally desperate Joey, languishing in 11th on the leaderboard, asking him for advice on how to get the thing to steer. Yet in remarkable contrast to previous years, he stood first and second respectively in the 250 and 125cc rankings. Maybe practice had gone too well in the two-stroke classes, for Joey seized at Hawthorn on lap one of the Ultra-Lightweight TT. He arrived back at the paddock, short of time and clearly pumped up, and proceeded to trash Ian Lougher's race record. Ten years after his first 250cc win, Joey clocked up another in what turned out to be a trouble-free, copy-book ride.

Joey had already come as close to winning the Formula One race as at any time since his heyday of the Eighties. Both he and McCallen were still beset by handling problems, with Joey also slowed by a loose intake ducting which was robbing the RC45 of 1000rpm on top speed. Nonetheless he led McCallen by seconds up to the first refuelling halt. Despite reattaching the plumbing, Joey could not overcome the narrow lead which McCallen had by now gained. McCallen rode with enormous guts on an ailing, evil-handling bike to win by 18 seconds.

With McCallen preferring to contest the Thunderbike class at the Italian Grand Prix, Joey was installed as favourite for Friday's Senior. After early opposition from Simon Beck's Ducati, he led all the way to the flag. A win in the premier class was special, but in McCallen's absence, slightly hollow.

The People's Champion

'He was the people's champion. He'd stroll out of the back of the garage with a fag on – and kick all our asses'
Roger Burnett, Honda team-mate

Old enough to be their father: Joey with a couple of young admirers – and Hislop and McCallen – after the 1991 Senior TT. (Don Morley)

By any standards of achievement Joey Dunlop was a superstar. Yet as an individual he combined the airs and graces of a postman with the preening self-regard of a monk.

'I'm just like any of the bikers who come to The Island to watch the racing,' he explained a few years ago. 'I just can't resist going out for another lap. I love the TT like I love motor

bikes and road racing.' The finishing line, not the bottom line, was what motivated him.

Famously, Joey remained loyal to Honda for the final two decades of his racing career, yet for more than half of those years he had no contract. His word was as good as his bond, and he expected the same from those he dealt with. If this was naïve, rarely was he ever exploited.

Bob McMillan describes those contract 'negotiations'. 'I used to meet him at Joey's Bar for a chat about the next season every January. When he was on his way to Australia for the last few years, he'd turn up with a little list and just wanted to know he was getting what he needed for the TT and the rest of the year. There was nothing in writing. Ever since I'd got involved in 1987, our contract was always a handshake. He'd just say, "that'll do, Bob."'

If Joey's loyalty to Honda was legendary, he was noted, too, for never forgetting a friend, or a favour. 'I still like to get involved with the people who helped me when I had nothing,' he once said. And there can be very few Irish racers of recent years who Joey hasn't loaned essential parts – anything from a gasket to a complete engine. Of course it wasn't wise to push it too far. Joey was 'a bit taken by surprise' to be promoted from MBE to OBE in February 1996. Some years later he was asked what the letters stood for. 'Owen Borrows Everything,' he replied with a grin, of his friend and protégé, the late Owen McNally.

Brother Robert has his own perspective on Joey's later career. 'Joey was fortunate that he had a god-given talent, something that he didn't have to work hard at. Fellows like Roger Marshall used to train really hard and couldn't understand how Joey could go pubbing, arrive ten minutes before the start, throw his leathers on and win. But lately he realised that as you get older, even he had to try harder.'

Ian Switzer, Embassy Irish 500cc champion back in 1983, has an abiding mental picture of Joey at Yugoslavia's Rijeka circuit in 1979. 'We'd just arrived and there he was – set up with his old 408 Mercedes, with a tent lashed to it and held down by old starter motors. He was living on toast and tins of baby potatoes, because he could recognise the picture on the

Happy in his work. (Stephen Davison – Pacemaker)

In 1993 Joey adds the official Freedom of Ballymoney to the freedom of Donegal he had always enjoyed. (Clifford McLean)

can. He'd work all night, get a wake-up call about 15 minutes before practice, tape these bits of plastic oil can to his knees and off he'd go. The rest of the paddock was pretty flash and professional, but Joey was just doing it his way.'

'His way' was what made Joey special. Like the first time he was confronted by a factory tyre technician way back at Dundrod in 1980. 'Och, put a slick on the back and a wee bit of hold [tread] at the front.' This was the same man who used to stay with his family at 34 Groudle Glen Cottages on the Isle of Man. Often, of an evening, the living legend and folk hero would stroll down to the Manx Arms for 'a swallow' and a game of darts with the locals. Almost as accomplished with the arrows as with a racing bike, he once hit three 180s in an evening. He was just one of the lads.

'He had no airs or graces in the early days,' says Linda, 'and he never got any. We'd go out for a meal and he'd be recognised, and he really couldn't understand why. He was the most down-to-earth person I ever met.'

Although the romantic notion now is that the special affection for Joey sprang from such ways, it was his riding which first endeared him to the Irish public. Nick Jefferies remembers 'this scruffy lad with amazing talent' at the Skerries races in 1975. 'Everyone was warning us about this man Joey and how we'd have to go some to beat him. The other thing I remember was an invitation to join race officials in the stewards tent for a wee drink *before* the last race. Irish racing was like that then.'

'You see all this stuff about his compassion, about Bosnia and so on, but the bottom line was his riding ability,' reckons Paul Farmer, cousin of the late Mark. 'You were in awe of the man. During the Eighties in Northern Ireland, the Troubles were bad, but for two days each year – the North-West and the Ulster – he was the one Irishman who was a match for the English and foreign riders. And everyone would turn up to see this one man. I don't think a lot of his fans knew or cared what religion he was.

'My brother wasn't at all interested in motor-cycle racing, but he'd go to watch Joey, and my mum was the same. Even my gran used to listen out for him on the radio. Anyone else was just a rider. Joey was an institution.'

'It didn't matter who or what you were to Joey,' recalls Billy Nutt about a race meeting near Riga. 'The Latvian Minister for Sport wanted to meet him, but he'd already arranged to go out for a bite with some of the lads, so that's what he did.' There was no rudeness or lack of respect. Had the Minister got in first, he'd have been the one sharing dinner, but rank

bought him no special privileges with Joey.

In motorcycle racing, the top wages – and the biggest egos – can be found in Grand Prix paddocks. Joey had little use for either. In his 48 years he only ever bought one new car. And even though he could probably have had a new one every few months from Honda, he never so much as asked, preferring a van or his elderly Mini. 'Last year he went to the North-West 200 in this battered old red Mini,' grins Linda. 'He learned me one valuable lesson – never worry

Opposite: As if The King of the Roads would ever voluntarily go away. (Don Morley)

Buckingham Palace, February 1996, and King Joey is promoted to OBE by his Queen. (Joey Dunlop Family Collection)

Sammy Graham wheels Joey's bike towards the start of the 1996 Senior TT. On the big bike, Phillip McCallen once again had the edge. (Don Morley)

Burnett. 'He might have cut it as a rider, but all the media stuff – that was miles scarier to him than Bray Hill flat-out could ever be. The rest of us did the whole image bit because we wanted to earn more money. On one level we felt Joey could destroy the whole thing with one picture or one interview. But the truth was that he was more popular than the lot of us put together. And he hated being confronted by the public, although he loved kids. He'd sign autographs for them all day.'

'You couldn't run Joey,' explains long-time manager and friend Davy Wood. 'You had to go with him. You could try to steer him gently in some directions, but that's all. He had his own way of doing things. Trying to get him to do the corporate thing at TT wasn't easy. He'd say "Look, do you want me to get these bikes going, or do you want me to shake hands and meet people?"'

In a racing career even longer than Joey's, Mick Chatterton came to know Himself well. 'He could give the wrong impression – that he couldn't be bothered. But it wasn't that at all. He was shy, yes, and his mind was sometimes just elsewhere. When you got his confidence, he was a fantastic bloke.'

For an Englishman, in particular, getting Joey's confidence wasn't the easiest of tasks. Chatterton – himself one of the most easy-going of racers – reckoned he truly broke the ice only in 1998 when 'he needed help to unload the van after losing his finger at Tandragee. Then last year we're walking back to the paddock after a plug chop, and he asked how the wee bike was going. When I told him not so well, he said to drop by at the garage. When I got there, he beckoned me over to his little corner, and started pulling boxes from under benches – a cylinder and head, exhaust, piston. "Put those on," he said. The Honda brass just looked on in amazement. The last time I saw him was when I took the parts back after the race.

'But it wasn't just his riding. The man himself was special, although it's hard to define that too. He didn't talk much and didn't appear to have much of a personality – but he'd got the biggest personality you'd ever seen.

about what people say, just get on with it.' No public figure was ever so lacking in spin.

'I don't think Joey ever wanted to be a GP rider, to be in the shop window,' reckons Roger

'I knew Hailwood pretty well, and this might sound stupid because their backgrounds couldn't have been more different, but they were very similar. Neither could stand the bullshit, neither knew what a lot of the fuss was about, but both could walk into a place and lift the atmosphere just by being there. And both would always accept being beaten by a better guy on the day.'

Mechanics, too, warmed to Joey. You can talk to any of Joey's many helpers, most of them volunteers, and hardly any can remember him ever saying 'thanks'. That isn't to say he was ungrateful, just that he communicated it in different ways from the rest of us. And, most of all, there was something about him – somewhere between an aura and an almost child-like vulnerability – that provoked people to help.

Even Linda encountered the same: 'He didn't let on, but he noticed. Three years ago Joey and the girls arranged a secret holiday for me and him to the Seychelles after our 25th anniversary. He must have heard me cooing over the place when it was on some holiday show on TV. That was typical Joey.'

'One of the nicest people I've ever worked for,' reckons Slick Bass, who has spannered for many of the top men. 'He wasn't major chatty, but he was very thankful for what you did for him. Even though we were being paid by Rothmans for doing it, he didn't expect it. He seemed to prefer to feel as though we were working for him because we were mates.'

Bertie Payne witnessed the phenomenon year after year. 'It didn't matter where you went, people just flocked around him. He was everybody's hero. He'd never complain, unless someone came to him in the last seconds before a race, then he might snap a wee bit.'

'I've seen him angry,' admits Bob McMillan of Honda Britain. 'You knew when he was because you just kept out of his way. He wouldn't kick things around, just go very quiet and intense. People would part before him as he walked through the paddock. Mind you, he was that revered they'd usually do that even if he wasn't in a huff.

'And he would very rarely turn up on schedule. You had to go and get him. For the Honda day at Laxey I would turn up at his cottage in Groudle Glen at 2.00pm in the afternoon. He was usually still in bed after a celebratory

Joey enjoys a well-earned 'swallow' after taking yet another TT win, his 20th, in 1996. (Allsport)

Opposite: Joey catches Michael Rutter on the road at Tower Bends, one of the most picturesque sections of the TT course, during the 1997 F1 race. (Don Morley)

Tell him he was too quick to ticket – and wish him luck in the races

session. I'd sit on the bike outside, waiting while he chased his trainers around the bedroom. But when you finally got him there, it was worth it. Just by being there he made everyone's day.'

In other circumstances the Year 2000 TT might have been remembered for a typical Joey piece of comedy in the opening practice session. Having completed a lap on his 125, he jumped onto the 250 thinking it was fuelled and ready to go, disappearing down the Glencrutchery Road before his crew could put him right. At the Verandah the bike coughed and died. Joey coasted to the Bungalow, still high on Snaefell Mountain. Undaunted, the Irish legend somehow contrived a length of plastic hose and borrowed fuel from a marshal's CBR900 Honda. 'Won't you need oil in that?' queried an amused onlooker. Without further ado, Joey unscrewed the fork drain plugs of his 250, and added it to his booty. 'That story got back to the pits before him,' said Ernie Coates, shaking his head.

Then there were the illegal sorties onto the public roads, with which any red-blooded road rider can identify. 'Before the North-West in 2000 the Vimto Hondas turned up and needed testing,' remembers Sammy Graham. 'I reckoned the Finvoy road would be perfect. Joey sends me up in a car to check it's clear and who should I meet at the end but the police? So back I go to tell Joey. He's gone. "He left after you on the bike", they tell me.

'Two seconds later my phone rings. "Did you meet the police?" asks Joey.

'Did you? Where are you?' I ask him. "I'm hiding at your place."

'Then the police arrived. "When Joey turns up," they said, "tell him we passed him going the other way at about 150mph, but he was a bit too quick to give a ticket. And wish him all the best for the races."'

1996

The 1996 season wasn't a vintage one all round for Joey but it was, beyond any ques-

A group of Swedish biking pilgrims enjoying the craic – and the black stuff – in Joey's Bar in 1996. (Mac McDiarmid)

tion, Honda's TT. Having continued to support TT racing long after other manufacturers had quit, they collected no fewer than six solo victories. Only the single cylinder class eluded them, and they could justly claim to have been undefeated in that, for no Hondas competed.

All six wins also went to Ulster. Phillip McCallen became the first man ever to win four TTs in one week. And Joey – who seven years before had tipped the Portadown rider as the man most likely to follow in his footsteps – took the other two. Narrow advantages over Jim Moodie in the Lightweight 250cc event and over Gavin Lee in the 125cc race brought Ballymoney's best-known publican wins number 20 and 21 respectively. Yet again Joey's practice form – sixth in the Lightweight, fourth in the 125 – gave little hint of the success ahead.

After a win on the 250 in the post-TT Steam Packet races, Joey climbed into his van and headed off to Riga, imperial capital of the Latvian Republic, for a round of the 'Pure Roads' series. Organised by Billy Nutt who also ran the Ulster GP, the series had rounds in Estonia (Tallin), Germany (Fromberg) and Belgium (Mettet). For Joey this was paradise – back to his roots, contesting events all over the place and working on his own race bikes from the back of a truck, just like any ordinary cash-strapped rider.

'He preferred just to go on his own,' says Billy. 'He'd generally drive at night and sleep during the day – get up and jump in a lake for a swim. He was interested in war graves and would visit all sorts of stuff like that. He enjoyed his own company.'

After wins at Riga in the 125 and 750cc classes, Joey was dicing with a local hot-shot named 'Agras' when he lost the 250's front end braking into a tight downhill bend. The spill left him with a fractured shoulder blade and damaged finger. 'It was my own fault,' he admitted after they'd strapped up the shoulder. 'But I'll be back. It's just a scratch.' Although he raced late in the season, reconstructive surgery forced a two-month lay-off which effectively ended his chances that year.

1997

Since stopping smoking, Linda remembers, Joey 'began to put on weight but looked after himself more, walking and running. He was never a fitness freak but always pretty fit. Queens University tested him and said he had the fitness of a 35-year-old.'

Victory in the 250cc Lightweight TT pushed Joey's all-time tally to 22 wins, and in the process proved that the youngsters still had some way to go. Two seconds adrift at the half distance pit stop, McCallen was pushing to make up for time lost changing a rear wheel when he crashed out at over 120mph at Quarry Bends. Joey struggled with a sliding rear tyre on the final lap, but was by then over 40 seconds ahead of the field. Those trailing him read like a who's who of 250cc TT racing, with

Ian Lougher, John McGuinness, Sean Harris and Gary Dynes battling for the minor places.

Although the rest of TT week would be a disappointment, his win was an emphatic response to suggestions that he might be over the hill. For good measure he took the 250cc class at Dundrod, and wrapped up the 'Pure Roads' series once more.

1998

This was a season which began with Joey, refreshed after wintering in the heat of Australia, raring to show the young pretenders yet again that he was The Man. And it was supposed to be a celebration of Honda's 50 years on the Isle of Man. Instead, the TT paddock looked more like an army field hospital.

Joey signing racing photographs at the 1998 TT. He had to be pretty busy not to have time for younger fans (Double Red)

Opposite above: Ian 'Lucky' Lougher chases Joey's ailing 125 through Sulby Bridge on the way to winning the 1997 Ultra Lightweight TT. (Don Morley)

Opposite below: A painful memento of Tandragee, May 1998. (Double Red)

In action on the RC45, 1999. (Stephen Davison – Pacemaker)

Opposite: *Gerard Deegan raises funds for cancer charity with the help of a lap on the back of King Joey at Dundrod, 1999. (Alastair McCook)*

Linda and long-time supporter Ernie Coates look on as Joey speaks to his friend Simon, Castrol World Superbike mechanic, about his last Formula One win. The author can be seen between them, in the background. (Stephen Davison – Pacemaker)

The injury roll call began on 2 May at Tandragee when Joey was spat off his 125 dicing with brother Robert and Owen McNally. His injuries included a broken left hand and collarbone, cracked pelvis and the loss of the end of his wedding ring finger. At around the same time, Phil McCallen damaged three vertebrae in a crash at Hampshire's Thruxton circuit. Two weeks later Robert broke his fibula at the North-West 200 – ironically having spent much of the intervening time struggling to be passed fit to ride following his 1994 TT crash. Another TT winner, Jim Moodie cracked a bone in his wrist at the same event and was doubtful until the last moment. In the event only McCallen failed to race.

Joey and Linda at the Ballymoney civic reception after the 2000 TT. It would prove a fateful day. (Joey Dunlop Family Collection)

Sammy Graham vividly recalls: 'I remember him lying under a sheet at the hospital, really upset, saying "Me hand's wrecked". At the TT the problem was that the empty finger of his glove was flapping, and hurting the stump like mad. We had to tape it back to the palm.'

To have turned up for practice at all showed just how much guts and bloody-minded toughness matter, and that Joey had both in abundance. If he needed an excuse not to fight the pain over 150 miles of the toughest course in the world, the Manx weather duly obliged. It blew and it poured. But far from giving it a miss, the man better suited to an orthopaedic bed than a racing bike, in conditions more suited to yachting, confounded everyone by splashing through the puddles to win his 23rd TT. Fittingly, this gutsy performance was witnessed by Soichiro Honda's widow, who had not been on The Island since 1964.

In pain or not, Joey Dunlop still knew how to out-fox his opponents. The race was scheduled to be run over three laps, which for most riders meant one pit stop. Whilst many of his rivals elected to pit after lap one, Joey held on in worsening weather. Sure enough, the same Manx gods who had overseen many of his 47 years came through for him again as low clouds rolled in, visibility dropped, and the race was reduced to two laps. Joey didn't pit. The rest did. Joey won. Or maybe there was another reason. With the fastest lap of the race and a comfortable 43-second lead over his nearest rival, Joey's wet-weather smoothness would probably have given him the win anyway.

'That was one of the most incredible rides ever, in the worst conditions I'd ever seen,' reckoned Mick Chatterton, a TT racer since the Sixties. 'I saw him in the paddock before, and he said if it stayed that wet he wouldn't be racing, and look what he did. And it wasn't just a missing finger – his hand was horribly swollen. I asked after if he'd had many problems. He just said "Och, I didn't go fast enough to have any problems". And me, Simmo, Moodie, and lots of others, we'd all pulled in. Incredible.'

Joey pronounced himself fit for The Island but too sore to ride anything bigger than a 250. Even this was progress far beyond the pessimism of just a few weeks before, as

Private Joey

'There was a bit of a gypsy in him … as long as he had what done him, he never asked for any more.'

Linda Dunlop

In an age when people become famous simply for being famous, or for preening on the pages of *Hello!* magazine, Joey Dunlop could see no logical connection between talent and fame. The adulation he received constantly surprised and embarrassed him.

He was at heart a reclusive man. In private he cherished solitude just as much as in public he prized winning on the race track. His idea of an extravagant trip, according to Linda, was 'three sleeping bags, three fishing rods and a van with two of the boys to Donegal. And every year after the Southern 100 we'd go away for four weeks' driving holiday to France, Spain, Portugal, Italy, Switzerland – all over the place, all in one go. We'd do some camping, some hotels. Joey just loved to drive. There was a bit of the gypsy in him. He could have lived alone on top of a mountain. He'd have loved to have gone back to a time with no electricity or whatever.'

Donegal was Joey's sanctuary. The hills and glens of Ireland's north-west corner was where he went for space and time alone. Sometimes there would be no particular reason to get away. At others, there would, as when his racing friend Owen McNally lay critically injured after crashing out of the Ulster in 1999. 'That hit him hard,' said Andy Inglis, shaking his head. 'Whenever anything like that happened, Joey'd take off to Donegal, and that's what he did in his little red Mini with a mattress in place of the passenger seat. Owen was on life support at the time, but Joey would never go near the hospital.'

Linda, Joey and family near the Honda TT workshop on Douglas Quayside, IT 1991. (Phil Masters)

Joey ponders his future. The prospect of what might one day replace racing probably scared him more than racing itself ever did. (Allsport)

Opposite: Fogarty tracks Joey through Quarter Bridge in 1991, in his first truly 'voluntary' outing on the CBR600. Joey placed a very respectable sixth. (Don Morley)

Other than his local church on Garryduff Road, hospitals played as big a part in Joey's adult life as any other institution. And yet he never really got the hang of them, or of broaching the anxiety they contained. 'He found it very difficult to go into hospitals,' explained his cousin and sometime spannerman, Jackie Graham. 'Even when Willie or Robert were in, it was the same. He said to me when Willie was ill, years ago, "I cannae even ask about me da – I have to wait to hear the rest talking about it."'

Odd? Yes. But then 'Nobody really knew Joey,' reckoned Sammy Graham, who knew him all his life. 'You just got glimpses.

'When we were racing he never said much. You just had to leave him be when he had his race head on. He'd come in and couldn't tell you how, say, the 250 had been. We'd go for a couple of drinks and relax, and he could usually tell you then. Or he'd write it down on a sheet of paper and leave it in the garage.'

'Even at home he was very quiet,' agrees Linda. 'He'd come in, have a shower then sit in front of the TV. Or play Nintendo – he loved that. You could hear that wee Mario all the time. He was that same person from the word go, and never really changed at all.'

So here was a simple, enigmatic man, simultaneously innocent enough to be in thrall to Super Mario, yet sophisticated enough to have a high-tech global corporation at his beck and call.

Younger brother Robert says, 'He wouldn't do anything bad to others, and he'd assume

Opposite: *'Take that, little brother!' The King is back on his throne, taking his 14th TT win, the Ultra Lightweight in 1992.* (Don Morley)

The Dunlop clan gathered to celebrate Joey's Freedom of Ballymoney in 1993. Left to right, rear: Julie, Linda, Louise (Robert's wife), Robert, Donna; middle row: Willie, Joey, Joanne and May; front: Gary, and Richard. (Clifford McLean – Pacemaker)

they wouldn't to him. And he was superstitious. He had this idea that if you told a lie, it'd somehow come back to haunt you. He'd rather say nothing.' As with many racers, superstition extended to his racing kit. The T-shirt had to be red and the left glove absolutely had to go on first. 'If you gave him his gloves in the wrong order, he'd just leave the right one lying there on the tank.'

There was a puckish side to the man too. The 'rock jumper' of Joey's youth kept a twinkle in his eye, and 'loved to play wee pranks,'

laughed Bertie Payne. 'Even at Tallin, when John Harris arrived he was met at the airport by a policeman telling him Joey couldn't meet him because he was in gaol for drunk and disorderly. And all the time Joey's just around the corner, giggling like an eejit … but he was a marvellous person to be involved with too.'

Nick Goodison, who shared a room with Joey whenever they travelled during 1988, also remembers the long boozy conversations, about the strangest things, deep into the small hours. 'And he'd always have some project in

Joey and Andy Inglis get stuck into the RS250. For Joey, practicality came first. In the early days he'd think nothing of draining his engine oil into a silver trophy if nothing better was to hand. (Stephen Davison – Pacemaker)

He preferred working as his own mechanic

Never the best early riser, Joey gets ready for practice at the North-West in 1993. (Stephen Davison – Pacemaker)

Opposite: *Almost caressing the wall at Sulby Bridge – scene of his only TT crash – on the way to an emotional Senior TT win in 1995. (Phil Masters)*

By no means dour amongst friends, Joey enjoys a laugh at Tandragee in 1994. (Stephen Davison – Pacemaker)

With the great Geoff Duke, three times a Senior TT winner and six times World Champion, on the Senior rostrum, 1995. (Phil Masters)

Opposite above: *Joey's personal fan club – his family – on the road down to Joey's Bar prior to Joey's personal Silver Jubilee in 1995.* (Joey Dunlop Family Collection)

Opposite below: *Cameras a-go-go, as ever. With daughter Joanne, then five years old, at the 1995 TT.* (Phil Masters)

the garage. That year it was his 125. He loved it – much more than the 250. Spent endless time working on it. Robert came to a lot of meetings with us that year. They'd spend endless hours, by candlelight in paddocks, discussing 125s.'

Even when working with factory technicians, Joey had the same combination of curiosity and scepticism. He once ambled into the Honda workshop in the middle of the night, when HRC technicians were preparing his RVF for the following day's race. Joey wanted to see *inside* the bike to satisfy himself about something or other. Astonished, the HRC men stripped the RVF for inspection by Himself.

'You wouldn't think it to look at him,' maintains Nick 'but he was a big, big thinker. I remember at Montjuich after about three laps of practice, he told me there'd be trouble at this particular corner – and that's where Rutter got hurt. He was always doing that sort of thing. He seemed to see things others didn't.'

Joey preferred working as his own mechanic, a tribute to the instinct for engines he developed as a child. As with Willie before him, this grew into the most dauntless self-reliance. Early in his career, when his van had wrecked its crankshaft climbing an Alpine pass, 'Joey not only produced a crankshaft from under the passenger seat, but proceeded to fit it in the snow'. He also created what was reputedly 'the fastest truck in Ireland', a Mercedes 408 with 3.5 litres of Rover V-eight shoehorned inside.

Inevitably this independence sometimes led to things that would have horrified the boffins at HRC. They'd spend months and millions of yen perfecting some component for the tuning kits on his two-strokes, only for Joey to fill it with Araldite and start all over again. Or for a missing cylinder to turn up in the sand pit beside Joey's Garryduff home, where the kids found it an ideal sandcastle mould.

JOEY AND THE MEDIA
'Tell them boys nothing'
Joey's advice to Willie on dealing with the press

Joey didn't much trust the press. At heart, he had as little use for the media as he did for celebrity status and all its trappings. The principal

exception to this not unreasonable prejudice was big Norrie White, former *Motor Cycle News* road race reporter. An imposing, no-nonsense Scotsman who towered above every race paddock, Norrie had known Joey since covering the major Irish meetings even before his first TT win, and would be the one journalist in whose company he felt comfortable for the rest of his career.

Norrie was fortunate in that he and Joey had a major shared interest other than racing, and that was bars. Now if 'Joey's office' was the beer tent behind the TT grandstand, Norrie's place of work was The Saddle pub on Douglas Quayside – which just happened to be the nearest amenable watering hole to Joey's workshop. They spent

many an hour rubbing elbows on the Saddle bar.

'Joey sometimes looked a fool,' boomed Norrie in his Dumfries brogue, 'but he was razor-sharp. The first story I did was a comparison between him and McCullough – two racers who couldn't have been more opposite.

'When I first met him he was having his dinner – a tin of beans. He lived quite frugally.'

Joey never lost his taste for beans – or his suspicion of the media. He wasn't openly antagonistic, he just didn't see the point. And, as Castrol Honda press officer Chris Herring observed, the tension worked both ways. 'I've never seen anyone look more uncomfortable than Joey whenever we staged a photo session.'

Equally, as Linda points out, 'he didn't like

Joey's front wheel paws the air powering out of the Gooseneck on his way to victory in the 250cc Lightweight TT 1997. (Double Red)

anything written about him if they hadn't got their facts right'. Although Joey would be the last to notice, the problem was that he scared many reporters half to death – and most of the rest couldn't understand a word he said. Getting the 'right facts' on Joey wasn't always the easiest of tasks.

A reporter on a local newspaper once handed Joey a camera as he set off on one of his mercy missions to Eastern Europe. 'Take a few pics of the kids and I'll do a wee story when you get back,' said the hack. On Joey's return, the reporter asked if he had his camera. 'I have,' replied Joey. 'But I didn't bother taking any pictures. I don't want any publicity if you don't mind.' It probably wouldn't have mattered if the recipients of his charitable efforts wanted publicity. Quite possibly, they craved it. But for Joey, being private came first.

Sometimes, of course, Joey watched, rather than starred on, television. Like most racers, he was a glutton for televised racing. 'We used to watch a lot of World Superbike races on TV,' remembers Linda. 'I always rooted for Aaron Slight, Joey for Foggy. He was also a huge admirer of Kenny Roberts and Mick Doohan.'

Nick Goodison says that Joey 'held Ray McCullough in such esteem, had massive respect for him. He was on a pedestal that even the likes of Gardner couldn't get on.' Ayrton Senna was another of Joey's heroes. On one of his charity sorties, he made the pilgrimage to

With brother Robert, himself five times a TT winner and Joey's greatest rival on the 125. (Stephen Davison – Pacemaker)

There were times for laughing, and times for deep thought. (Stephen Davison – Pacemaker)

Opposite: *The start of the 1998 250cc Lightweight TT, undoubtedly one of Joey's finest rides. Note the 'empty' finger strapped up for action.* (Mac McDiarmid)

Imola to pay his respects at the spot where the Brazilian motor racer died.

But even when he was in the spotlight, avoiding the media could have a recreational edge. Dubliner Eddie Laycock laughs as he remembers Joey being pursued by the press after losing out to the Bimotas at Assen in 1987. 'He escaped into our van – with two mugs and a bottle of vodka. He was supposed to get home on the Thursday, but I think he got there the following Tuesday.'

Mainly, his attitude to publicity was the same as his take on fame. One of his nieces, Margaret's daughter, once featured in a television documentary, together with uncles Joey and Robert. During filming Margaret commented on how long everything seemed to take, and of being fed up with the constant gaze of the cameras. 'Now you know how it is for me all the time', responded Joey with feeling.

Joey's own kids seemed to take celebrity status in their stride. 'I never knew any different,' reckons Julie, his eldest daughter. 'It all seemed completely normal.'

'Mind you she was spoiled rotten,' chimes in Linda. 'For a long time she was the only child. She had a great lifestyle going to all the races, meeting people like Freddie Spencer and Barry Sheene.' Julie objects, with a chuckle. 'My favourite was Kevin Schwantz,' she insists.

Rex Patterson, headmaster at Ballymoney High School, remembers the time when 'Julie came to me, asking for a holiday in term-time because her "daddy couldn't get away in the summer". I was reluctant, but gave her an exercise book and made her promise to keep a diary, with pictures. And she did. The most memorable part was in Spain. She wrote: "It was strange. As we went along, no-one knew Joey. And then we came near a race track and everyone cheered and waved."'

JOEY AID
'I saw the troubles on television and decided to help out'
Joey Dunlop

Despite his best efforts, Joey's one-man missions to Eastern Europe became quite well

known – even to Royalty, for his OBE was in recognition of the charity work. But this was only part of the story. Locally Joey was active in school fundraising, motivational visits to sick patients, and almost anything involving children. 'You probably won't have heard of these,' explained the Rev John Kirkpatrick, biker, fan and man of God, 'because the man himself preferred it that way. In fact you would have heard of none of it if the Queen hadn't seen fit to take note.'

A racing fan for long enough to 'remember the Tiger Cub and the Suzuki,' John Kirkpatrick has been chaplain to racing's Ulster Centre since 1993. Now based in

Portrush, he got to know the Dunlop family after taking over the Garryduff ministry in 1987. The church itself, built by local people with stones laboriously carried from the fields and river banks, could almost be a metaphor for Joey's self-sufficient approach to life.

'When I arrived,' John continues, 'he wasn't a regular churchgoer, but we had something in common – the bikes – and could chat. Sometimes he'd sit there and say nothing, others he'd chat away quite happily.' He described one occasion when there'd been some dispute in Joey's Bar about religion – what it was for, whether it worked – and Joey took the simple and direct approach in inviting

In practice on the 250 in 1998 – a far cry from the diabolical conditions in which Joey would win his 23rd TT. (Mac McDiarmid)

'my minister', the Rev John, down to the bar to answer the doubters.

'Willie got a wee bit argumentative,' John remembers, 'but Joey said not to worry, Willie didn't mean half of what he said. He was really concerned for my feelings. The next Sunday he arrived at the church – accompanied by three pews-full of his mates who'd been at the pub. I've never heard of that in any other church, and maybe only Joey could have done such a thing.'

For John, two more of Joey's qualities stand out. 'He avoided controversy and disagreement … walked away from it whenever he could. And he never had money, and never seemed to worry about it. It just wasn't that important to him. He'd have told you exactly how much he had if you'd have asked.'

Joey described how his charity mission began after he was approached by a Romanian refugee pleading for help with shipment of relief supplies. Transport was something Joey understood so, when he 'saw the troubles on television and decided to help out', the job was on its way. 'The food and clothes were donated locally,' Joey explained later. 'I drove around the area collecting them and set off when the van was full.'

'My first connection,' explains John Kirkpatrick, 'was in trying to help Joey with

Joey ponders a problem on the RC45 with Sammy and former Norton man Brian Crichton. (Clifford McLean – Pacemaker)

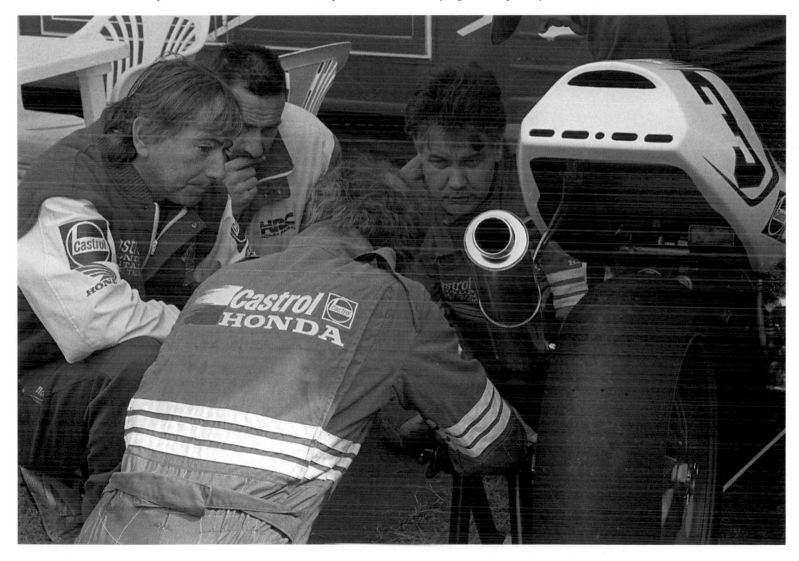

Joey looking pensive at Aghadowey, March 1999. (Alastair McCook)

carrying 70 tons. Then off he went, as though he were going to Belfast for the day. He just drove and drove and drove. It was mid-winter and must have been bitterly cold out there. Diesel freezes. He didn't come back to any sort of fanfare and didn't expect any. Some people tried to make a story of it, but not Joey. He just got on with his life.'

On the way home Joey dropped in on John Harris, his sponsor with the CBR600. 'The truck was a hoot,' remembers John. 'Kitted out like you wouldn't believe. He had a huge oil-fired central heating tank as an extra diesel tank. He'd done what he'd done, but you could tell he was itching to do more. My wife, who hadn't met him before, said he was a true Christian. He used to cuss and swear, but he didn't have a bad bone in him.'

Joey's second trip took him to a camp for refugees from the Balkan conflict in Hungary. 'This time we used the church hall to store stuff. When it was full he just bunged it in the van and drove off. These are risky places and the name 'Joey Dunlop' wouldn't mean much out there – although in a way Joey probably felt comfortable with that.'

When pressed, Joey would describe some of his adventures, such as being 'arrested at gunpoint on the way back from Albania for not having the correct documents. They wanted £25 for me to cross the checkpoint but I wouldn't pay. I gave them some racing stickers and motorcycling papers. The chief of police happened to be a motorsport fan, so he wrote me a letter allowing me to continue.'

In some of these places, you couldn't depend on such good fortune. People were shot for simply being in the wrong place. Sometimes, Joey admitted with typical understatement, he was 'a bit scared. Although I live in Northern Ireland I am out in the country and mostly away from The Troubles, so seeing a gun is still a shock.'

Further trips followed, to Albania, Bosnia and Romania again. Apparently the Romanians have a saying: 'Some people come once, but not many come twice'. Joey was one of the few.

paperwork for his first trip, to the Romanian orphanage, in 1990 – just pragmatic help, trying to get him organised. He had his race van and a trailer, vastly overweight. He must have been

Will He, Won't He?

'There was something inside me telling me he ought to stop – I told him I'd pay him not to race at the TT. But, to be honest, I doubt he ever would have. He'd always have had a 125 to take to Estonia or somewhere.'

Bob McMillan, Honda race boss

If there was one issue that occupied the Dunlop mind in later years more than almost anything else, it was the thorny matter of retire-ment. It had been on the agenda – the media's agenda, if not Joey's – since his Brands Hatch crash of 1989. By then he was already 37 years

Rounding Quarter Bridge on Bertie Payne's RS250 on the way to winning the 1995 Lightweight TT. (Phil Masters)

Opposite above: *The 250cc pack screams away from the line at the North-West 200, 1997. In a typically tight slipstreaming battle, Joey could finish only ninth.* (Phil Masters)

Opposite below: *A relaxed-looking Joey with his compatriot and old rival Steve Cull at the North-West 200, 1997.* (Phil Masters)

Joey sloshing through the puddles on the way to finishing fourth at Cookstown in April 1996. (Mac McDiarmid)

old, an age when most other riders certainly would have thought of trading race bike for pipe and slippers. But not Joey. No way. 'The big factor is enjoyment,' he told me after recovering from that crash. 'I've actually started enjoying my racing at the TT like I never have before. Many's the time that the bike is all set up and ready to race. But I can't resist taking it for another lap. I just love riding round The Island that much.'

Five years on, and the message was the same. 'No, I'm not ready to disappear just yet. I still enjoy racing, especially the great feeling you get when you cross the finishing line in first place. And if I gave up, I wouldn't know what to do at weekends. The time for me to retire will be when I can't concentrate on going fast any more – when I start thinking about my family and how dangerous racing is. But I can't see that happening yet.'

Even a decade later, the same old passion was still there. 'I love racing and everything about it,' he said after his final, glorious triple win, 'especially at the TT. The TT has always been the highlight of my year, it's special ... I know I can't do it for much longer. So long as I

feel fit and I'm competitive I'll keep racing … maybe I should only be riding in the smaller classes now.'

Then he added: 'The pressure of riding in the Rothmans Honda team of the 1980s isn't there any more but the physical demands are higher now. So I suppose it gets easier to cross the line in fifth or sixth place and accept that that was all I could do on the day, but I still want to win – that's the hardest part to work at.'

As ever, Joe's message was clear: a definite maybe.

During the latter half of the Nineties, no interview with Joey failed to ask when he planned to retire. He became bored, not to say irritated, with the question. But it was something which he sometimes asked himself. Or Linda. 'He'd ask me my opinion,' nods Linda, 'but I'd always tell him he had to decide for himself. I knew how much he loved it. But it wasn't something we sat and discussed as a big issue.

'Maybe he'd have retired if he'd had a terrible bad year. The only time I heard him say he wasn't going to race again was after Merv [Robinson] was killed in 1980. After he won at the TT [the next month] I remember him sitting in the bath, crying his eyes out, saying "This one's for Merv". There were a lot of emotions – happy and sad. Over the years he always felt really sad when other riders got hurt or died, but I suppose you think it isn't going to happen to yourself. That day at the TT he wore a red T-shirt – that became like his lucky mascot. He wore red T-shirts to race ever since.'

To most other onlookers, even close ones, the subject was taboo. May Dunlop has said that a couple of years ago she thought that, perhaps, Joey should retire. As with his father, though, the subject was never broached. Willie, of course, understood. 'For Joey, as for other riders, motorbike racing is like a drug,' he told Gail Walker of the *Belfast Telegraph* two

Opposite above: Pursued by Simon Beck, Joey revs the RC45 out of Gooseneck during a deeply disappointing 1997 Formula One TT. (Phil Masters)

Opposite below: With Owen McNally and John Creith inspecting the controversial Mill Road roundabout before the 1998 North-West 200. Twelve months later Donnie Robinson would die there, and two months after that McNally lost his life in the Ulster GP. (Alastair McCook)

Joey relaxed and raring to go in September 1998 at Carrowdore – one of his favourite road circuits. (Alastair McCook)

months after his son's death. 'It's an addiction. Once they start they can never quit. It's such an adrenalin rush. Stopping didn't come into it for Joey. It wasn't even a subject that I ever discussed with Joey. Not once. There was just an understanding, if you like, between us that he was going to keep on racing.'

For a few old hands it was a subject to be laughed about, at least superficially. 'We used to joke about retirement – I will when you do sort of thing,' chuckles Mick Chatterton. 'But Andy [Inglis] and Willie Fulton told me, three or four years ago, that he'd said he'd race until the Millennium.' Yet the Millennial season was a particular worry, as Bertie Payne recalls: 'He was worried about this year, said it was his 31st – his unlucky number – and no way of getting around it. Even if he took a year off, the next one would still be Number 31.'

There can be no doubt that Joey actively contemplated quitting racing. He just didn't know how to do it, or what might take its place. Ray McCullough describes a question as poignant as any in racing: 'In later years he used to ask me, "How did you stop racing?" I don't think he knew how to pack it in.' As long ago as 1989 he was facing the dilemma. 'I don't know what I'll do when I stop racing' he admitted over a beer in Joey's Bar. 'It's a bit of a worry to me.'

There were other indications too. In 1998 Joey organised a show of his trophies and memorabilia at the same Ballymoney Leisure Centre which is now named after him. During the 2000 TT week he arranged a similar display at Summerland, on Douglas seafront. What made him do that? Whilst neither event said unambiguously that Joey was about to retire, they were suggestive of punctuation marks being drawn on his career. He was due to be guest of honour at the 2001 Manx Grand Prix. And for years the TT Riders' Association – which he'd joined in 1980 – had been asking him to become President, but the prospect of standing up and making a speech terrified the life out of him. Finally he bit the bullet and accepted – but never lived to make that speech.

There were other changes too. The hair was strikingly greyer, and shorter. And, where once a tab dangled from his lips, now a pair of specs sat on the end of his nose. It was just one more sign that the body was getting older. 'I canna see with 'em, and I canna see without,' Joey used to complain. Others, though, remarked on his invigoration. 'I'd say he was enjoying his racing more,' reckoned Jim Dunlop, 'since he stopped smoking and started taking some exercise.'

Certainly the old fella had roared into 1999, winning on the RC45 first time out, and mixing it with the youngsters in a manner reminiscent of former glories. However the North-West 200 echoed to previous tragedies when Donnie Robinson – Joey's sparring partner from the early Eighties – came out of retirement only to die at the controversial new roundabout at Mill Road.

Although Joey seemed up for it, the TT was a disappointing affair that year. The opening race achieved infamy less than a mile from the start when Paul Orritt crashed his 900 Honda at Bray Hill on lap one. Surprisingly – thankfully – Orrit's injuries were not grave, but the race was red-flagged.

In the restart Iain Duffus again took an early lead, only to be overhauled by Joey and David Jefferies on lap two. Jefferies, drew ahead when Joey suffered a sloppy pit stop to replace a near-shredded Michelin. Faced with a 14-second deficit with just one lap to go, Joey charged to his fastest-ever TT lap at 123.06mph. Unfortunately, Jefferies went frac-

Opposite: 'Now where did we put those extra horsepower?' Willie and Joey Dunlop ponder the bike at Killalane, near Dublin, in 1998. (Alastair McCook)

In 1998 Joey organised this glittering display of trophies and memorabilia at Ballymoney Leisure Centre. (Clifford McLean)

Joey sits on his 1977 TT-winning 750 Yamsel at his exhibition in Ballymoney. (Stephen Davison – Pacemaker)

tionally quicker still, to win by 15.8 seconds. This would be the closest Joey would come to victory all week.

Ironically, the seeds of Joey's fabulous Year 2000 TT triple were sown in that disappointment. 'The RC45 had been incredibly difficult to get right for The Island,' admitted Bob McMillan, 'and we never had access to the full factory kit for those TTs. But I think he'd have won on it in 1999 if we hadn't cocked up the pit stop. He showed then that he still had it in him to win, but we let him down. After that, I think he worked harder – mentally and physically – building himself up for the 2000 TT.'

At 47 years of age, and with ten more TT wins than any man in history, Joey had little to prove. But just in case, in August he put in one of his finest performances to beat Jefferies and Duffus at the Ulster Grand Prix. 'A superb win, after a crap start,' reckons Bob McMillan. 'You've never seen a crowd so happy.' But you ain't seen nothing yet.

He showed he still had it in him to win

The Dunlop clan in the mid 1990s: Clockwise from top left: Linda, Willie, May, Joey, Richard, Julie, Joanne, Donna. Gary is missing. (Stephen Davison – Pacemaker)

Chapter Fifteen

V for Valedictory

'Joey wondered what the Japanese might make of 'this wee grey-haired man jumping on Aaron Slight's bike'
Linda Dunlop

To Honda, as to Joey, the TT was everything. 'The TT hadn't been the biggest thing in the world for the past 10 years,' explained Bob McMillan, 'but Honda – both in

Japan and in Britain – wanted to back Joey there, and the TT was Joey's main thing too. I wasn't bothered about what Irish races he did. I never expected him to do a lot at the North-

Surrounded by typically magnificent Manx scenery, Joey hustles his 250 into Keppel Gate in the barren year of 1999. (Mac McDiarmid)

Skerries, 1999, where Joey won the main event, smashing the lap record by over 2mph. Not bad for a 47-year-old father of five. (Mac McDiarmid)

Opposite: Road racing is not like Grands Prix, on two wheels or four. At corners such as Glasshouses on the Skerries circuit, you can get this close to the action. (Mac McDiarmid)

West because he never really liked the place, and over the last decade he didn't really shine there. My main interest was the TT – to make sure he had all the bikes he needed, via Andy [McMenemy] and Bertie [Payne] with the 125 and 250, and John Harris with the 600.'

For the larger classes, Honda's original plan was to provide Joey with a modified 900cc FireBlade road bike to take on the Yamaha R1 that had romped to victory in 1999. Joey tried what was more-or-less a production-spec FireBlade at an early season Irish meeting, but was far from impressed. Plan B was to borrow the Honda SP-1 normally ridden by James Toseland in UK Superbike races.

Joey first sampled the kitted SP-1 at Cookstown, in Vimto's sparkling livery. 'He really took to the bike,' remembers Bob McMillan, 'coming from the second wave to finish second. You could see that he loved it. Then he went out on his brand-new 250, and was leading by about 15 seconds in the wet when he fell off going into the right-hander after the start. The throttle had fallen off, and he'd been holding it on for god-knows how many laps. They had to disqualify him when he picked up the bike and finished, but he went mad – said he'd never been disqualified before.'

Later Joey tested at England's Cadwell Park,

Joey slings a leg over an SP-1 for the first time at Cookstown … (Stephen Davison – Pacemaker)

He was more professional, spending more time at the gym

Opposite: *… he really took to the bike.* (Alastair McCook)

TT 2000, and Joey makes final adjustments before another practice lap. (Gavan Caldwell – Pacemaker)

He expected to do well and was disappointed

Opposite: *Perhaps pondering what they thought of 'this wee grey-haired man jumping on Aaron Slight's bike'.* (Gavan Caldwell – Pacemaker)

'He seemed to see things others didn't.' Joey in reflective mood. (Gavan Caldwell – Pacemaker)

taking along Robert who had volunteered to help him at the TT. Robert had his own take on Joey's Year 2000 mind-set. 'He was different – riding harder. He won on the 125 at Tandragee. When he tested at Cadwell, it never stopped raining but they couldn't get him off the bike. He was flying – faster than Jim Moodie. He'd never done that on a short circuit in the wet for years. He knew he was on it. He said to me, half joking, "Maybe I'll have a go at the Supercup next year."' In Supercup the median age is about 25, going on 12.

However, the North-West, with its endless flat-out straights, was a different proposition from the tight Lincolnshire circuit. The kitted SP-1 was outpaced. 'By the North-West,' Robert remembers, 'he was more professional, spending more time in the gym. He was expecting to do well and was disappointed with how he'd gone – with how the bike had gone – although he never pushed himself at the North-West and rarely went really well there.'

Bob McMillan picks up the story: 'Before he got the SP-1, when it all looked like turning sour, Joey phoned me from Ireland after riding what was more-or-less a proddy 'Blade. He said Honda was being made to look a laughing stock. He was seriously unhappy and took himself off to Donegal for three days. He was in no mood to talk to anyone. Then he rang me. I'm on the M5, and my mobile phone rings. It's Joey and he's seriously unhappy.

'I'll never forget it'. He said: "This is supposed to be my last year and now it's ruined", because he could see that the bikes he had then weren't capable of winning the TT. He didn't use the word retirement and I took him to mean that this would be his last TT, but I was so startled I missed my turning and ended up heading down the M4 to Wales.

'As soon as I got back to the office I e-mailed Japan, told them Joey was thinking of retiring and didn't have a competitive machine. Lo and behold, back came an e-mail offering one of the World Superbike engines, forks, almost everything to make practically a full works bike. To help set the bike up, we ended up with top HRC technicians, two Showa engineers, and Simon Greer, Slighty's mechanic. And he was

potent combination, the same wasn't so obvious to everyone. 'At the TT there was a senior HRC man with the bike,' grinned Bob McMillan. 'He didn't know what the TT was about and obviously wondered why they'd gone to so much bother to put this grey-haired old Irish bloke on one of their bikes. But Joey had never given up on winning another big bike TT, so I knew he'd put in the effort if the chance came. I think over the last five years he'd got himself fitter, almost as though he'd been building himself up for one last big effort.'

The rest, as the cliché goes, is history – a piece of history pregnant with joy, and poignancy and sorrow. 'If' is probably the most commonly used word in motorcycle racing, and certainly the most futile. If only …

If only Joey had paid heed at the jubilant mêlée that was the TT prize-giving, when Bob McMillan publicly suggested he'd like Joey to retire. When Ballymoney threw Joey a civic reception, complete with open top double-decker bus doing 'a tour of the town, just like Man United,' he repeated the same suggestion, with Ulster's Ministers for Sport and Tourism looking on. Joey's response was memorably described as 'a very loud smile'.

'I'd said the same privately to Linda after each of his TT wins last year,' admits Bob. 'I suppose I was the only one being negative, in a way.

'After the civic reception me and Joey talked for about 1½ hours in his pub about how we could make plans for his retirement – if he did retire. I told him I'd pay him not to race at the TT, but to come and help if he wanted. He said "The day I ride for money will be the day I pack in." What he was saying was that money wasn't the reason he rode in the first place, so how could money possibly persuade him *not* to race? I smiled to myself. I knew I couldn't win.

'But we talked about how he could maybe turn his pub into a museum, or establish one somewhere else, possibly Bushmills. We finished drinking at about 4.15 in the morning, after a last "one for the end of the bar." It would be their last shared "one for the end of the bar".

Irish, so he could communicate with Joey as well.'

'After that,' chuckles Davy Wood, 'people were arriving on planes with factory bits in their pockets. He was so loyal to Honda, and they to him. Who else would they have produced a factory SP-1 for?'

If Joey knew he and the factory SP-1 were a

Farewell

'I just knew him as Joey, round and about, you know. It wasn't until he was gone that I realised what a star he'd been.'

One of Joey's fans in Ballymoney

When Joey Dunlop died on Sunday 2 July 2000 at an obscure road race meeting in the pine forests on Estonia's Baltic coast, it was a multi-dimensional tragedy. The loss belonged to the Dunlop family, to Joey's friends, to racing and to the whole of Ireland. But the context in which it occurred was also desperately cruel.

Joey practising on the 125 at Tallin on the day before his death, at the corner which would claim his life. (Hannu 'Lexi' Lehtonen)

(Pacemaker)

(Shane Ellis/Sportbike)

(Shane Ellis/Sportbike)

(Pacemaker)

(Shane Ellis/Sportbike)

(Pacemaker)

(Pacemaker)

(Pacemaker)

They all adored Joey and he was at home there

The Estonian road races are held on the 3.7-mile 'Pirita-Kose-Kloostrimetsa' circuit, a couple of miles up the coast from the medieval walled city of Tallin. Joey turned up for the meeting a week early and spent the interlude based in the igloo tent provided by the organisers, chilling out. Saturday, the first race day, was mainly dry, but Joey won the 600 race in a rain shower. It was the first time John Harris, who'd flown in for the weekend to watch, had seen Joey win an international event on one of his bikes. Joey had encouraged him to go, then secretly paid for his flight from the UK.

It was again wet – 'water bouncing off the track' – for Sunday's Superbike race. Using full wet tyres front and rear, Joey won again.

When the bikes lined up for the 125cc race 15 or so minutes later, the track was drying rapidly. In such circumstances tyre choice is always tricky, particularly on such a long track where conditions may vary considerably from place to place. Joey opted for a full wet front and an intermediate rear, nodding to John Harris after the parade lap that the combination seemed OK.

The crash happened three laps into the race, just as it began to rain again. Eye witnesses described the 125's rear wheel stepping out part-way through the last corner, a left-hand bend where the surface is quite flat and water tends to lie. Joey corrected the slide, but was by then running out of room. This was deep in the pine forest where there was no run off, and a crash was inevitable. Joey got rid of the bike, which wedged itself between two trees, snapping in two. Parts of the machine struck two spectators, but their injuries were mild. Joey struck another tree. He died instantly, although attempts at resuscitation were made as a matter of routine.

When checked out later, there were no indications that the Honda's engine had seized – an obvious suspicion in such an accident. Evidently no solo rider had been killed on the circuit since 1961. Wet or dry, you'd have put your house on Joey not being the next.

People have asked, angrily, 'what was he doing there?' and a few may be looking for someone to blame. It was typical of the man that he should race – as he had several times before – at such a backwater. Some years ago I visited the circuit. The local bike racing club was a poverty-stricken crowd enthusiastically racing anything with wheels – not unlike a grubby young fella from Ballymoney, on a battered old Tiger Cub, 31 years before. They clearly adored Joey, and he had seemed at home there: no fuss, just his bikes, a track, the fans, and something to contribute. As to blame, I imagine that the man would be horrified at the suggestion that responsibility lay with anyone but himself.

Joey's start money in Estonia was £1000. So he certainly wasn't there for the wealth, but when was he ever? He was there to get away.

The previous month, Joey's long-standing sponsor Andy McMenemy had taken his own life, following business problems. This was the most bitter of tragedies. A good and dear friend was dead. We can only imagine how Joey felt, but John Harris was with him when the news reached them the next morning. 'He was

Sports Minister Kate Hoey and Dr Ian Paisley MP were among the more than 50,000 mourners. (Shane Ellis/Sportbike)

stunned … just couldn't take it in. Why? Why? he kept asking.'

'Joey took his 125, John Harris's 600 and an RC45 lifted from the ceiling of Joey's Bar where it had been on display,' remembers Sammy Graham numbly. 'The bikes were loaded, with spares, a new primus stove, and tins of beans, because when Joey got going he wouldn't stop, just make himself something in the van.'

Davy Wood remembers with the same quiet horror 'the last time I spoke with Joey. It was in a pew at Andy's funeral. He said he didn't want to be talking about Andy, so he was pissing off away for a while. I remember Andy stepping in for Joey when everyone else thought he was finished, and I'll always be grateful for that.'

What Harold Crooks in the Irish *Sunday Life* called 'a summer of tragedy' continued on 13 August when a pile-up at the Monaghan road races claimed the lives of Gary Dynes and Andrew McClean. With road racing already in crisis, no sooner had September's Carrowdore races got an eleventh hour go-ahead than

Eddie Sinton crashed fatally, joining Ray Hanna – killed at the 2000 TT – on Tandragee's roster of woe. This was barely a year after the loss of Donnie Robinson at the North-West, and Owen McNally at the Grand Prix. Ireland grieved.

As so often, it was left to the widow to try to make sense of it, but no amount of waiting and worrying leaves you prepared, as Linda explained a few months later: 'When it happens to some other racing wife you wonder how they can cope. You have the worry at the TT … if they break down and go missing for a few minutes, you feel sick. This year, with him winning the three, you get back home and think that's your worry over for the year.

'You can be angry now, but you can't be angry for the past 30 years, because the past was good. Joey picked his sport. Unfortunately it took his life, but it gave him and us 30 great years. What makes me really angry is people who try to use his death to destroy the sport he loved.'

Floral tributes overflowed Joey's Bar onto the adjacent railway station. (Clifford McLean)

Borne by his two sons-in-law and brother Robert, Joey's coffin makes its sombre way along Garyduff Road in what amounted to an unofficial state funeral. (Clifford McLean)

On the world scale, motorcycle road racing is pretty small beer, yet Joey transcended that. His death was global news. The story was carried prominently on TV, on radio, in the *Washington Post, Las Vegas Sun*, and countless other newspapers across the planet.

At Dublin airport, a crowd greeted the aircraft returning Himself from Tallin. As the hearse bearing Joey's body arrived at the undertakers in Ballymoney in the small hours, the Town Hall bell struck three – his race number. Or so it is said. But, even if fanciful, the tale is no less moving for that.

Joey was buried at Garryduff Presbyterian Church where, just a couple of years before, he and Linda had re-taken their marriage vows. A state funeral in everything but name, the occasion was broadcast live on Irish national television, and attended by government ministers from London, Belfast and Dublin. Even at the sectarian battleground of Drumcree, a truce

was declared whilst the protesters remembered 'Yer Maun'.

Garryduff Road is a typically straight country lane undulating across the North Antrim countryside. It runs from Ballymoney, past Joey's old school and the leisure centre later named after him, by the Dunlop bungalow, on past Garryduff Church towards where the infant Joey first lived near Dunloy. On this same road Joey illicitly tested racing motorcycles. On 7 July 2000, as the cortège bore the coffin slowly by, it was tempting to imagine the ghostly wail of a racing two-stroke, but the murmur of mourners was the only sound.

It seemed like all of racing, and half of Ireland, gathered around the little church that day. Over the hastily-erected public address we heard Joey's daughter Donna read her poem of '... the yellow helmet shining bright ...' and people wept. Fifty thousand of us said goodbye. And thanks.

Endpiece

DADDY

by Donna Dunlop
read out by her at the funeral

To people you were a number one,
To me you were a daddy,
To people you were a quiet person,
To me you liked to party.

That smile of yours was real,
Nothing there was false,
The knight in shining armour,
Was always in a rush.

The yellow helmet stood out bright,
The number three there too,
The Honda always shone out light,
But you always remained true.

Now, I know why Jim called you the gurk,
On that face you had a smirk,
Up the paddock you'd go a walk,
But then the folk would start to gawp.

You hated the publicity,
You liked to go your own pace,
But the only thing I have to say,
I know you loved to race.

The racing was your life,
But you just couldn't stop,
But then again, why should you have done?
Because you were top of the plot.

The light is on,
Our hearts are pumping,
On the grandstand
We are jumping.

The only thing you ever wanted
Was another Formula One.
But you sure showed them you could do it,
By giving them your 24th win.

At the Ulster last year
There was an awesome vibe,
But you sure showed David Jefferies,
On the RC45.

Our lives will never be the same.
In our hearts you will remain,
Deep in thought and in our laughter,
Because we all know you were the master.

We never thought this day would come
When we had to say goodbye,
But the memories I have of you,
God, I wonder why.

You were simply the best,
Better than all the rest,
The only thing I have to say,
That's you, Sir Joey, all the way

THE ROAD RACER

by Bob McMillan
A tribute to the greatest road racer of them all – ever

A kind of madness, they call it 'Road Race',
Infects the minds and hearts of Racers.
The Racers' eyes look clear yet distant,
They speak of things so strange and different.
Of grunt and springs, of jets and settings.
They meet at night and talk and fix things.
Through the dark much mumbled chatter.
Dawn breaks, what's with the clatter,
With push and shove, bike barks to life
Midst smoke and dust and maybe strife.
Screaming, jumping and scaring cattle,
One last run and She's ready for battle.

The roads are closed and people do wait
In places good, to cheer on their mates.
One Racer arrives in 'nick of time'.
Paddock bustles with a tension sublime.
'Yer Maun' walks through with clear intent.
People part, His gaze fixed and set.
Respect for 'Himself' is clear to see,
For the quiet, shy man from Ballymoney.

Bob McMillan is General Manager, Honda Racing UK, and worked closely with Joey Dunlop for almost 20 years.

An extract from Bob McMillan's eulogy at the funeral

You know, Joey touched millions of people with his modesty, his humility and his humanity, and I'm sure he never knew – he never knew how great a star he was.

He was also a great fighter, as many of us know. Remember when he lost his finger before one of the TTs just a few years ago? He was riding hurt. Actually, he didn't think he could ride that weekend. He was really, really struggling, but he won the 250 race in the wet in front of Mrs Honda – and Mrs Honda's last time in the Isle of Man, I think, was 1964. His biggest worry though was not that he'd lost his finger, but that he couldn't keep his wedding ring on, because you know that Linda would give him stick if he hadn't got the wedding ring on, and that was his biggest worry!

And you know, there's another side of Joey that not everybody sees because when he had his 'race face' on and he was at the North-West or the TT or the Ulster, he looked a bit serious and a bit stern, but he was also full of mischief. You know, he went to Tallin, he went to that race, the last race, to relax and get away from things and do what he's always done, just be a bit of a lad really, and he invited John Harris over. John's supported him for the last ten years with his 600, and John arrived at the airport and a senior representative from the government came up to John and said, 'Mr Harris?' He goes, 'Yes'. He said, 'You're here to meet Mr Dunlop?' He goes, 'Yes'. He said, 'He's in gaol' and John goes, 'You're joking?' – and with that, Joey pops his head from behind the door. He was hiding round the corner and he just set him up really.

That was Joey! But then he won the 600 race, he won the Superbike race on the old RC45 that he's took off the roof of the pub yet again, and he was leading the 125, and that's how we'll always remember him.

Awards showered on Joey in his final racing season included:

Motor Cycle News Man of the Year (Birmingham ICC)
Guild of Motoring Writers Rider of the Year (London)
Texaco Sports Stars Award Rider of the Year (Dublin)
BBC Sports Star of the Year (Belfast)
Road Racing Ireland, Rider of the Year, and Enkalon Rider of the Year, presented by Sheene and Doohan (Belfast)
Irish Post Sportsperson of the Millenium

Bob McMillan with Joey at the Belfast Bike Show in 1999. (Stephen Davison – Pacemaker)

The Family thank you for your
expression of sympathy by your
presence here today.

You are warmly invited to join with
them for tea in the Church Hall
following the committal.

Funeral conducted by James McMullan & Son
22 High Street, Ballymoney

Garryduff Presbyterian Church

SERVICE OF THANKSGIVING

FOR THE LIFE OF

WILLIAM JOSEPH (JOEY) DUNLOP
O.B.E., M.B.E.

1952 - 2000

on

FRIDAY 7th JULY 2000

HYMN

I have a Shepherd, One I love so well;
How He has blessed me, tongue can never tell;
On the cross He suffered, shed His blood and died,
That I might ever in His love confide.

Following Jesus, ever day by day;
Nothing can harm me when He leads the way,
Darkness or sunshine, whate'er befall,
Jesus, the Shepherd is my All in all.

When I would wander from the path astray,
Then He will draw me back into the way;
In the darkest valley I need fear no ill;
For He, my Shepherd, will be with me still.

When labour's ended and the journey done,
Then He will lead me safely to my home;
There I shall dwell in rapture sure and sweet
With all the loved ones gathered round His feet.

HYMN

The Lord's my shepherd, I'll not want.
He makes me down to lie
In pastures green, he leadeth me
The quiet waters by.

My soul he doth restore again,
And me to walk doth make
Within the paths of righteousness,
E'en for his own name's sake.

Yea, though I walk through death's dark vale,
Yet will I fear no ill;
For thou art with me, and thy rod
And staff me comfort still.

My table thou hast furnished
In presence of my foes:
My head thou dost with oil anoint,
And my cup overflows.

Goodness and mercy all my life
Shall surely follow me:
And in God's house for evermore
My dwelling-place shall be.

Results

Isle of Man TT: J Dunlop awarded silver replica except (b) = bronze or where stated otherwise, * indicates record race speed

1976 TT

Joey's first TT. Prior to practice he had never seen the course before and plays 'tag' with faster riders to learn his way round.

Junior 350cc

1	C Mortimer	Maxton Yamaha	1:46:00.2	106.78mph*
16	**J Dunlop**	**Rea Yamsel**	**1:53:22.8**	**99.83mph(b)**

Record lap: T Rutter, Yamaha, 20:49.6, 108.69mph
Club Award: Cookstown & District MCC: B Guthrie, J Dunlop, C Junk

Riding with number 65, Joey posts a fastest lap at 22:08, 102.3mph.

Lightweight 250cc

1	T Herron	Yamaha	1:27:26.8	103.55mph

Fastest lap: Tom Herron, Yamaha, 21:27.8, 103.55mph

Starting number 68, Joey retires on lap one.

Senior 500cc

1	T Herron	351 Yamaha	2:09:10.0	105.15mph
18	**J Dunlop**	**354 Yamaha**	**2:17:49.0**	**98.55mph(b)**

Record lap: J Williams, 20:09.8, 112.27mph

Joey is a late entry, taking over Gordon Pantell's number, 44. Another bronze replica, in a race best remembered for John Williams' push-in on the final lap, when he ran out of fuel when leading by almost five minutes. Williams later takes Classic TT.

Classic

1	J Williams	Suzuki	2:05:33.0	108.18mph

Fastest lap: J Williams, Suzuki, 20:32.4, 110.21mph

J Dunlop retires on lap four when his Yamsel's crankshaft failed.

Production Race

1	B Simpson/	250 Yamaha	4:05:09.8	87.00mph
	C Mortimer			

Fastest lap: R Nichols, Ducati, 21:57.0, 103.13mph

Joey is paired with Billy Guthrie to ride a Yamaha RD400 in the 10-lap production event, but their machine expires in lap one with Guthrie riding. The bike has number 3, later to become Joey's own.

1977 TT

They say it takes at least three years to learn the course, but in only his second visit to the TT, Joey takes his first win and earns more prize money than he has ever dreamed of before.

Junior 250cc

1	C Williams	Yamaha	1:08:10.0	99.62mph
10	**J Dunlop**	**Rea Yamsel**	**1:11:32.2**	**94.93mph**

Fastest lap: I Richards, Yamaha, 22:18.8, 101.45mph

Joey wins his first silver replica. Fastest lap setter Ian Richards would later become a Castrol Honda mechanic.

Senior

1	P Read	500 Suzuki	1:45:48.4	106.97mph
4	**J Dunlop**	**350 Rea Yamsel**	**1:49:47.0**	**103.10mph**

Fastest lap: P Read, Suzuki, 20:30.4, 110.01mph

In misty, damp conditions the race is shortened from six laps to five. Joey is 12th after lap one, gradually making his way up the order to finish on the leaderboard for the first time. His fastest lap, over 105mph, is a personal best.

Classic TT

1	M Grant	747 Kawasaki	2:02:37.4	110.76mph*
7	**J Dunlop**	**351 Rea Yamsel**	**2:09:11.8**	**105.13mph**

Fastest lap: M Grant, Kawasaki, 2:04.4, 112.77mph

Joey gets under 20 minutes – 108mph – for the first time. But for stopping to adjust his chain, it could have been even better.

Schweppes Jubilee Classic

1	**J Dunlop**	**746 Rea Yamaha 1:23:10.6**	**108.86mph**

Fastest lap: J Dunlop, Yamaha, 20:24.4, 110.93mph

Joey takes his first race win, ahead of a Mr G Fogarty of Blackburn, father of Carl. Despite an early misfire, his opening lap is the third-fastest ever. And £1000 is by far the biggest prize of young Joey's life.

1978 TT

An anticlimactic TT for Joey, in a week best remembered for Mike Hailwood's stirring F1 win. But it is also a year of tragedy, with the deaths of sidecar aces Mac Hobson and Kenny Birch, and serious injury to factory Suzuki star Pat Hennen.

Formula 1

1	M Hailwood	864 Ducati	2:05:10.2	108.51mph

Fastest lap: M Hailwood, Ducati, 20:27.8, 110.62mph

Starting number 2 alongside the 888cc Honda Britain machine of 1977 winner Phil Read, Joey rides Dave Mason's 812 Devimead Honda, but retires on lap 5.

Joey on his way to claiming the 1000cc 'Superbike' race at the 1979 Ulster Grand Prix. Dundrod would usually be kind to Joey. (Clifford McLean)

Senior
1   T Herron   Suzuki   2:01:33.4   111.74mph

Fastest lap: P Hennen, Suzuki, 19:53.2, 113.83mph

Riding a badly jetting and misfiring RG500 Suzuki, Joey retires on lap 2.

Junior 250cc
1   C Mortimer   Yamaha   1:52:23.8   100.70mph
11 J Dunlop   Yamaha   1:56:40.0   97.02mph
12 M Hailwood   Yamaha   1:56:46.8   96.92mph

Fastest lap: C Mortimer, Yamaha, 22:10.8, 102.06mph

In this rain-delayed and otherwise disappointing race, Joey started 10 seconds behind Mike the Bike, overhauling him on the first lap to beat him by one place.

Formula Two
1   A Jackson   600 Honda   1:31:8.6   99.35mph
5   J Dunlop   550 Benelli   1:36:56.0   93.41mph

Record lap: A Jackson, Honda, 21:56, 103.21mph

The Benelli was due to be ridden by Snuffy Davies, but a late change brought Joey his best result of the week.

Classic
1   M Grant   KR750 Kawasaki 2:00:50.2   112.40mph

Fastest lap: M Grant, Kawasaki, 19:48.0, 114.33mph

Starting number 1, Joey tours back to the pits and retires on lap 3 when the exhausts of his 750 Rea Yamaha began to break up.

1979 TT
Another disappointing TT for Joey, de-tuned by tragic events at the North-West 200 just one week before, when Tom Herron and Frank Kennedy both crash out with fatal results.

Formula One
1   A George   Honda   2:02:50.6   110.57mph

Fastest lap: A George, Honda, 20:02.6, 112.94mph

Joey, ill-advisedly riding a cumbersome 896 Benelli Sei supplied by importers Agrati Sales, pulls out on lap 2.

Senior
1   M Hailwood   RG500 Suzuki 2:01:32.4   111.76mph

Record lap: M Hailwood, Suzuki, 19:53.2, 113.83mph

Riding Hector Neill's RG500 Suzuki, Joey retires on lap 3 after lying 11th after one lap.

Junior 250cc
1   C Williams   Yamaha   2:09:11.8   105.13mph*

Record lap: C Williams, Yamaha, 21:11.4, 106.83mph

Riding Sam Taggart's Yamaha, Joey runs out of fuel and retires on lap 6 after lying 10th the previous lap.

Formula 2
1   A Jackson   600 Honda   1:29:9.8   101.55mph
13 J Dunlop   597 Benelli   1:39:55.0   90.62mph

Record lap: A Jackson, Honda, 21:53.6, 103.40mph

Joey finishes but not even as quickly as the previous year's F2 race and fails to gain a replica.

Schweppes Classic
1   A George   998 Honda   2:00:07.0   113.08mph*
6   J Dunlop   750 Rea Yamaha 2:04:39.2   108.96mph

Fastest lap: A George, Honda, 19:49.6, 114.18mph

Highlight of the week is the stirring duel between Alex George's big Honda and Mike Hailwood's RG500 in the £30,000 Schweppes Classic, 'the richest race in the world'. Joey scrapes on to the leaderboard as George beats the old master by just 2.6 seconds.

North-West 200 wins
International Match race
NW200 race

Ulster Grand Prix wins
500cc
Superbikes

1980 TT
It's back to winning ways for Joey, in what he would many years later describe as the most satisfying result of his career – and one which showed just how crafty a racer he could be. But the death of Merv Robinson at the North-West 200 took away much of the shine at the time.

Talbot 500cc
1   G Crosby   500 Suzuki   2:03:52.2   109.65mph
9   J Dunlop   350 Yamaha   2:07:11.2   106.79mph

Fastest lap: S Woods, Suzuki, 20:19.6, 111.37mph

Starting number 5, Joey rides his 350 Yamaha rather than the 500-4 which had seized its gearbox at the NW200.

Junior 250cc
1   C Williams   Yamaha   1:28:34.8   102.22mph
12 J Dunlop   Yamaha   1:31:58.2   98.45mph(b)

Fastest lap: D Robinson, Yamaha, 21:39.4, 104.53mph

Twelfth place is worth just £50, barely enough to put new piston rings in the Yamaha.

Classic
1   J Dunlop   750 Rea Yamaha 2:00:29.8   112.72mph

Record lap: J Dunlop, Yamaha, 19:38.8, 115.22mph

John Rea's enormous 32-litre tank defeats Honda's expensive quickfillers in what second-placed Mick Grant (998 Honda) describes as the hardest race of his career. The £8,000 prize money is the stuff of dreams.

World Formula One Championship

Isle of Man TT: Joey does not compete

Ulster Grand Prix, 16 August
1   G Crosby   998 Suzuki   38:50.6   114.32mph
2   J Dunlop   998 Suzuki

Fastest lap: J Dunlop, Suzuki, 3:47.2, 117.27mph

The World F1 series comprises just two rounds, the Isle of Man TT and the Ulster GP. Joey does not contest the TT round, but places second on a factory Suzuki to shepherd Graeme Crosby to the title.

Final Championship Standings
1   G Crosby   Suzuki   27
2   M Grant   Honda   25
3   J Dunlop   Suzuki   12

Ulster Grand Prix wins
250cc
Superbikes

1981 TT
Joey's first TT as a factory rider, with the Honda Britain squad: no wins, but a first lap record in the Classic race.

Formula 1
1   G Crosby   997 Suzuki   2:01:28.8   111.81mph
3   J Dunlop   999 Honda   2:04:07.6   109.42mph

Record lap: G Crosby, Suzuki, 19:54.6, 113.70mph

Joey leads early on in his first TT as a factory Honda rider, but his bike goes sick, then he loses more time changing a wheel. The race is most notable for protests, with Crosby declared the winner from Ron Haslam 2½ hours after the finish.

Joey taking Hector Neill's RG500 Suzuki to victory for a memorable double in the Ulster GP, 1979. (Clifford McLean)

Joey shows off the latest Rothmans livery in 1985. (Don Morley)

Honda team boss Barry Symmons leans over Joey's shoulder after yet another Honda F1 win. (Don Morley)

Classic

1	G Crosby	998 Suzuki	1:59.34.8	113.58mph*

Record lap: J Dunlop, Honda, 19:37.01, 115.40mph

In the notorious 'Black Protest' race, Joey retires on lap 5 with a blown engine, having earlier run out of fuel and pushed in when chasing and passing Crosby on corrected time. But from Ballacraine to Ballacraine Joey averages 117mph: a sign of things to come. The race is the first six-lapper completed in under two hours.

World Formula One Championship

Isle of Man TT: see TT results

Ulster Grand Prix, 22 August

1	R Haslam	999 Honda	41:54.8	105.95mph
5	**J Dunlop**	**999 Honda**		

Fastest lap: R Haslam, Honda, 4:07.6, 107.61mph

Honda spent much of the season struggling to get the best out of their machinery, but Crosby was unstoppable, also winning the British F1 series by a mile.

Final Championship Standings

1	G Crosby	Suzuki	27
2	R Haslam	Honda	27
3	**J Dunlop**	**Honda**	**16**

North-West 200 wins
NW200 race

1982 TT

Again, no TT wins, but taking the world Formula One title – in front of his own fans – brings undiluted joy to Joey, and to Ireland.

Formula 1

1	R Haslam	999 Honda	1:59:50.6	113.33mph
2	**J Dunlop**	**999 Honda**	**2: 04:26.0**	**109.15mph**

Record lap: M Grant, Honda, 19:41.8, 114.93mph
Team Award: Honda: R Haslam, J Dunlop, J Elbon

Joey suffers handling problems and an engine that won't rev.

Classic TT

1	D Ireland	RG500 Suzuki	2:04.21.8	109.21mph

Fastest lap: C Williams, Yamaha, 19:57.0, 113.47mph

In a race of attrition, Joey leads early on, but the 1024cc RCB four slows, dropping him to sixth on lap five when his cam chain snaps at the Bungalow and he retires.

World Formula One Championship

Isle of Man TT, 5 June: see TT results

Vila Real, Portugal, 4 July

1	W Gardner	999 Honda	1:11:51.2	91.02mph
2	**J Dunlop**	**999 Honda**		

Fastest lap: W Gardner, Honda, 2:48.2, 93.32mph

Ulster Grand Prix, 21 August

1	R Haslam	999 Honda	38:02.8	116.72mph
2	**J Dunlop**	**999 Honda**		

Fastest lap: N Brown, 997 Suzuki, 3:45.6, 118.10mph

In a world F1 series expanded to include a non-UK round for the first time, three second places is enough to secure Joey his first world title. Joey also contests the MCN/Shell British Streetbike series on a Honda CB1100R. He looks set to win the final round at Brands Hatch, but slides off at Bottom Bend, leaving Wayne Gardner to win race and championship.

Final Championship Standings

1	J Dunlop	Honda	**36**
2	R Haslam	Honda	30
3	D Hiscock	Suzuki	26

1983 TT

Arriving on The Island with a beard and a new son, Joey records the first of many Formula One TT wins despite a practice week hampered by machine problems and bad weather. *Motor Cycle News*, on the other hand, headlines 'Dunlop's TT scorcher!'

IoM Formula 1

1	J Dunlop	850 Honda	1:59:06.4	114.03mph*

Record lap: J Dunlop, 19:33.6, 115.73mph
Team Award: Honda: J Dunlop, R Marshall, H Kerner

In what was to become a demoralising habit, Joey sets a lap record from a standing start, and is already 7 seconds ahead of the field at Ballacraine on lap one. By leading on all six laps he earns £10,250 prize money, a record for a TT race.

Senior Classic TT

1	R McElnea	997 Suzuki	1:58.18.2	114.81mph*
3	**J Dunlop**	**850 Honda**	**2:00:24.4**	**112.80mph**

Record lap: N Brown, 498 Suzuki, 19:29.0, 116.19mph

Run in place of the Senior, unforgivably abandoned this year. Struggling with handling problems and later fuel supply problems, Joey leads early on but is eclipsed by big Rob Mac. Ulsterman Norman Brown runs out of fuel after setting the record lap.

World Formula One Championship

Isle of Man TT, 4 June: see TT results

Assen, Dutch TT, 25 June

1	R McElnea	997 Suzuki	46:50.56	97.82mph
2	**J Dunlop**	**850 Honda**		

Fastest lap: R McElnea, Suzuki, 2:53.97, 98.77mph

Ulster Grand Prix, Dundrod, 20 August

1	J Dunlop	920 Honda	53:45.60	107.38mph

Fastest lap: J Dunlop, Honda, 4:02.01110.10mph

McElnea pushes hard, trailing Joey by just two points going into the final round. At Dundrod, McElnea and Grant lead off the line, but Joey hurtles past into Rushyhill corner and clears off at 'suicidal' speed.

Final Championship Standings

1	J Dunlop	Honda	**42**
2	R McElnea	Suzuki	35
3	R Marshall	Honda	26

North-West 200 wins
NW200 race
500cc race

1984 TT

Joey arrives on The Island buoyed by a double win at the North-West 200 to take a second successive Formula 1 win. But McElnea has the edge in Senior and Classic races.

Formula 1

1	J Dunlop	Honda 750 RVF	2:01:37:0	111.68mph

Record lap: J Dunlop, Honda, 19:32.0, 115.89mph

Four stops, two in the pits and two on the road to kick the exhaust away from the rear tyre, can't stop Joey winning again.

Senior
1 R McElnea   497 Suzuki   1:57:26.2   115.66mph*

Record lap: J Dunlop, 498 Honda, 19:06.4, 118.47mph

Joey sets a new lap record on every one of the first five laps, only to retire with a broken crankshaft on lap 6 at Mountain Hut when leading by 40 seconds. His new outright lap record will stand until he breaks it himself in 1988. McElnea laps at 118.23mph, to take Suzuki's seventh consecutive Senior TT.

Junior 250cc
1 G McGregor   250 EMC   2:03:57.6   109.57mph*

Record lap: G McGregor, 20:23.0, 111.06mph

For the second time in a week, Joey retires on lap six, at Les Graham Memorial, when he runs out of fuel whilst lying second to Graeme McGregor's EMC.

Premier Classic
1 R McElnea   998 Suzuki   1:56:58.2   116.12mph*
2 J Dunlop   920 Honda   1:57:12.4   115.88mph

Record lap: R McElnea, 19:19.6, 117.13mph

Riding the factory 920 endurance motor, a weary Joey loses out by 14.2 seconds to Rob Mac. 'I don't know how anyone rides them for 24 hours,' he says after.

Production Class B
1 T Nation   750 Honda   1:06:25.2   102.24mph*

Record lap: T Nation, 750 Honda, 102.97mph, lap time n/a

Joey retires his 748 Honda on lap two with 'tyre problems' as does team-mate Reg Marshall. Team manager Symmons indicates they wouldn't be expected to contest the proddie event in future.

World Formula One Championship

Isle of Man TT, 2 June: see TT results

Assen, Dutch TT, 30 June
1 R Marshall   750 Honda   1:00:29.19   94.52mph
2 J Dunlop   750 Honda

Fastest lap: R Marshall, Honda, 2:22.55, 96.26mph

Vila Real, Portugal, 15 July
1 R Marshall   750 Honda   1.09:25.4   94.20mph
2 J Dunlop   750 Honda

Fastest lap: R Marshall, Honda, 2:43.59, 95.95mph

Ulster Grand Prix, Dundrod, 18/19 August
1 J Dunlop   750 Honda   50:31.0   114.28mph

Fastest lap: J Dunlop, Honda, 3:46.1, 117.74mph

Zolder, Belgium, 2 September
1 M Pajic   750 Kawasaki   1:09:03.00   82.84mph
2 J Dunlop   750 Honda

Fastest lap: M Grant, Suzuki, 1:50.27, 86.45mph

In a season of sometimes bitter rivalry between team-mates Dunlop and Marshall, the Lincolnshire man loses out cruelly when his gasket blows in the final round, gifting Joey the title in a manner unsatisfactory for both.

Final Championship Standings
1	J Dunlop Honda	66
2	R Marshall Honda	54
3	T Rutter Ducati	36

North-West 200 wins
MCN Masters race

Ulster Grand Prix wins
250cc
500cc

1985 TT

Joey's TT gets off to the most infamous of starts when the fishing boat 'Tornammona' sinks en route to Peel. Luckily no-one is hurt, although eight bikes – none of them Joey's – go down with the vessel. Practice week is further marred by gales, but Joey emerges from it all with a record-equalling three wins.

Formula 1
1 J Dunlop   Honda RVF   1:59:12.0   113.95mph*

Record lap: J Dunlop, 19:26.6, 116.42mph

Despite a split exhaust and a minor rear brake problem, Joey wins from Tony Rutter by no less than five minutes, 40 seconds: 'It seemed a long race because I was so far in front and had to just reel in the laps.'

Junior 250cc
1 J Dunlop   247 Honda   2:03:35.0   109.91mph*

Record lap: B Reid EMC, 20:11.8, 112.08mph
Team Award: Honda: J Dunlop, S Cull, M McGarrity
Club Team Award: Mid-Antrim MC: J Dunlop, C Law, G McDonnell

Joey's specially enlarged fuel tank had spent several days at the bottom of Strangford Lough and began leaking just before the start, requiring a precautionary fuel stop. He inherits the lead when Brian Reid runs out of petrol two miles from the finish: 'the jammiest win I've ever had'.

Production Class B
1   M Grant   GSX-R750 Suzuki 1:05:04.6   104.36mph*
22 J Dunlop   NS400 Honda   1:09:01.8   98.38mph

Record lap: G Williams, Suzuki, 21:22.2, 105.93mph

By now Joey had a distinct aversion to road-legal tyres, and cruised around in a race he'd been told in '84 he wouldn't be riding.

Senior
1 J Dunlop   750 Rothmans   1:59:28.2   113.69mph
                Honda

Fastest lap: R Marshall, Honda, 19:30.2, 116.07mph
Team Award: Honda: J Dunlop, R Marshall, R Burnett

Roger Marshall missed a first TT win by an agonising 16 seconds as Joey, using his slower spare engine, enjoyed 'one of the easiest rides I've had on The Island, hardly any incidents at all.'

World Formula One Championship

Isle of Man TT, 1 June: see TT results

Assen, Dutch TT, 29 June
1 J Dunlop   750 Honda   1.06:36.07   85.84mph

Fastest lap: K vd Endt, Kawasaki, 2:30.94, 90.91mph

Vila Real, Portugal, 7 July
1 J Dunlop   750 Honda   1:10:01.02   93.41mph

Fastest lap: J Dunlop, Honda, 2:43.85, 95.79mph

Montjuich Park, Barcelona, Spain, 13 July
1 J Dunlop   750 Honda   1:18:53.77   78.73mph

Fastest lap: J Dunlop, Honda, 1:48.07, 82.13mph

Ulster Grand Prix, Dundrod, 17 August
1 J Dunlop   750 Honda   50:26.3   114.45mph

Fastest lap: J Dunlop, Honda, 3:48.1, 116.81mph

Hockenheim, W Germany, 29 September
1 J Dunlop   750 Honda   55:17.07   110.52mph

Fastest lap: J Dunlop, Honda, 2:15.21, 112.96mph

Having won every one of the championship's six rounds, Joey is described, by Nick Harris in *Motocourse*, as 'the greatest pure road racer of all time' in an article regretting the lack of recognition he had thus far received in what the English like to call 'the mainland'.

Joey at another successful TT in 1987. Later that year he'd lose the world title he'd almost made Ireland's own. (Phil Masters)

Race commentator Fred Clarke nobbles Joey at Donington Park, 1988. (Phil Masters)

With Steve Hislop, 'the young pretender', after placing second to him in the 1991 Senior TT. (Don Morley)

Joey tucks in to take TT win number 15 in 1993 on Andy McMenemy's 125. (Don Morley)

Final Championship Standings

1	J Dunlop	Honda	90
2	M Grant	Suzuki	40
3	G McGregor	Suzuki	32

North-West 200 wins
250cc (race 1)
NW200 race

Ulster Grand Prix wins
250cc
500cc
TT F1

250cc British Grand Prix: Silverstone 4 August
In a race won by Honda's Anton Mang Joey places 10th to earn his only grand prix world championship points.

1986 TT

Joey's TT is marred when brother Robert is badly injured after crashing at Cronk Urleigh in Tuesday's Formula 2 event.

Formula 1 TT, IoM

1	J Dunlop	750 Honda	1:20:09.4	112.96mph

Fastest lap: J Dunlop, 19:51.6mph, 113.98mph

In a race postponed to Monday and reduced to four laps because of Saturday rain, Joey won by a minute from Geoff Johnson, to take the lead in F1 world championship from Anders Andersson. The Swede, contesting his first TT, finished a brave 12th for no points.

Junior 250cc

1	S Cull	249 Honda	2:03:54.0	109.62mph

Fastest lap: P Mellor, EMC, 20:19.0, 111.42mph

Unusually, Joey had topped the practice leaderboard with a lap at 110.97mph, 25 seconds faster than Steve Cull. More unusually still, in the race he recorded his only TT crash, at Sulby Bridge on lap one whilst leading by seven seconds. He re-mounted only to retire with a broken exhaust after lap four. The race is bleakly remembered for the death of Gene McDonnell, who hit a pony at Ballaugh.

Production Class C

1	G Padgett	RG400 Suzuki	1:05:56.6	102.98mph
4	**J Dunlop**	**NS400 Honda**	**1:06:55.4**	**101.48mph**

Fastest lap: G Padgett, 21:40.6, 104.43mph

Joey cruises through yet another production race, in which Gary Padgett beats Malcolm Wheeler by a mere 1.0 seconds. Tragically, Padgett dies in a road accident nine days later.

Senior

1	R Burnett	500 Honda	1:59:09.8	113.98mph
4	**J Dunlop**	**750 Honda**	**2:01:21.2**	**111.92mph**

Fastest lap: T Nation, Suzuki, 19:25.4, 116.55mph

Riding his F1 machine, Joey suffers major handling problems, and loses three minutes in the pits replacing a steering damper bolt. Burnett wins after inheriting the lead from Marshall and then Nation.

World Formula One Championship

Misano, Italy, 6 April

1	M Lucchinelli	750 Ducati	1:48:11.85	90.14mph

Fastest lap: J Dunlop, 750 Honda, 1:24.3, 92.56mph

Hockenheim, W Germany, 4 May

1	J Dunlop	750 Honda	52:38.50	110.58mph

Fastest lap: J Dunlop, 2:14.09, 113.25mph

Joey 'in a class of his own', but still behind Anders Andersson in championship.

Isle of Man TT, 31 May–6 June: see TT results

Assen, 23–28 June

1	J Dunlop	750 Honda	59:39.17	95.84mph

Fastest lap: N Robinson, 750 Suzuki, 2:19.83, 98.14mph

Kevin Schwantz was second.

Jerez, Spain, 13 July

1	P Iddon	750 Suzuki	1:11.35.67	79.07mph
5	**J Dunlop**	**750 Honda**		

Fastest lap: not given.

Vila Real, Portugal, 20 July

1	J Dunlop	750 Honda	1:09:33.25	94.03mph

Fastest lap: J Dunlop, 2:42.34, 96.69mph

Imatra, Finland, 3 August

1	J Dunlop	750 Honda	1:0:12.1	93.49mph

Fastest lap: J Dunlop, Honda, 1:55.83, 95.60mph

Ulster GP, Dundrod, 16 August

1	N Robinson	750 Suzuki	52:16.9	110.42mph
2	**J Dunlop**	**750 Honda**		

Fastest lap: N Robinson, Suzuki, 3:57.9, 111.99mph

As Formula One prepares to give way to Superbikes, the series sees better fields at more rounds on more varied circuits than ever before. Joey comes from behind after running out of fuel in a 'Misano disaster' to clinch his fifth and last world title.

Final Championship Standings

1	J Dunlop	Honda	93
2	P Iddon	Suzuki	61
3	A Andersson	Suzuki	58

North-West 200 wins
NW200 race

Ulster Grand Prix wins
Superbike race

1987 TT

While HRC soldiered on with Freddie Spencer's increasingly bizarre behaviour in grands prix, Joey delivers them yet another TT win. Formula 1 victory puts Joey alongside Giacomo Agostini and Mike Hailwood as the only man to win the same TT race in five successive years.

Formula 1

1	J Dunlop	750 Honda RVF	1:58:04.4	115.03mph*

Record lap: J Dunlop, Honda, 19:15.4, 117.55mph

'King Dunlop's Master Class'. Initially three seconds down on Mez Mellor, Joey has to dig deep in what is 'as hard an F1 TT as I've had', but wins by a comfortable 51.8 seconds, with a lap record 11.2 seconds inside his old mark.

Junior 250cc

1	E Laycock	250 EMC	2:05:09.2	108.52mph
8	**J Dunlop**	**247 Honda**	**2:08:03.4**	**106.06mph**

Fastest lap: S Hislop, Yamaha, 20:18.0, 111.51mph

Joey starts on intermediate tyres only for the rain to hold off, and is further hindered by a broken exhaust. In an otherwise good race for the Irish, Dublin's Eddie Laycock posts his first TT win, ahead of Brian Reid – after Steve Hislop seizes when leading by miles on lap five.

Production Class B

1	G Johnson	Yamaha FZR750	1:01:45.0	109.98mph
18	**J Dunlop**	**Honda VFR750**	**1:04:51.2**	**104.71mph**

Record lap: T Nation, Yamaha, 20:16.6, 111.64mph

Joey failed to gain a replica.

Senior

1	J Dunlop	500 Honda	1:30:41.2	99.85mph

Fastest lap: J Dunlop, Honda, 21:22.6, 105.08mph

In appalling conditions, in a race already postponed one day and reduced to four laps, Joey is masterly in recording his 10th TT win after pressing Mez Mellor into sliding out. Says Mellor's manager, Mick Grant: 'We were on the right tyres and he was on the wrong ones, yet he still won. Magnificent.'

Production Class C
The race is the first to be cancelled since the TT races began in 1907. Joey qualifies in fifth place at 104.04mph in a top 12 entirely composed of the new Honda CBR600.

World Formula One Championship

Misano, Italy, 20 April
1	P Iddon	750 Suzuki	1:48:02.2	90.27mph
3	**J Dunlop**	**750 Honda**		

Fastest lap: R Marshall, Suzuki, 1:23.48, 93.45mph

Hungaroring, Hungary, 3 May
1	V Ferrari	Bimota	1:21:39.31	73.31mph
8	**J Dunlop**	**750 Honda**		

Fastest lap: R Marshall, Suzuki, 1:59.16

Isle of Man TT, 30 May: see TT results

Assen, Holland, 25 June
1	V Ferrari	Bimota	59:02.05	96.79mph

Fastest lap: D Tardozzi, Bimota, 2:19.28, 98.46mph
J Dunlop DNF.

Ulster GP, Dundrod, 15 August
The meeting is abandoned after the fatal crash of Klaus Klein.

Sugo, Japan, 30 August
1	K Magee	Yamaha	1:22:57.82	83.95mph
12	**J Dunlop**	**Honda**		

Fastest lap: n/a
Mick Doohan was third.

Hockenheim, W Germany, 20 September
1	V Ferrari	Bimota	51:28.26	113.09mph
4	**J Dunlop**	**750 Honda**		

Fastest lap: V Ferrari, Bimota, 2:12.68, 114.45mph

Donington Park, England, 27 September
1	P Iddon	750 Suzuki	1:08:58.82	86.98mph
3	**J Dunlop**	**750 Honda**		

Fastest lap: R Marshall, Suzuki, 1:41.87, 88.34mph

In what was in effect a forerunner of World Superbikes, Virginio Ferrari wins the championship without once racing on public roads. Imatra is dropped from the series when it fails to meet safety standards, and Vila Real is bizarrely shelved when a snap general election intervenes.

Final Championship Standings
1	V Ferrari	Bimota	49
2	**J Dunlop**	**Honda**	**46**
3	P Iddon	Suzuki	43

North-West 200 wins
750cc Production
Superbike race
NW200 race

1988 TT

Motor Cycle News reports that Joey is 'miffed' not to be getting special factory tackle: 'The Superbike is two stone heavier and that'll make all the difference.' Thus handicapped, he records a TT triple for the second time in his career.

Formula 1
1	J Dunlop	750 Honda	1:56:50.2	116.25mph*

Record lap: J Dunlop, Honda, 19:05.8, 118.54mph
Team Award: Honda: J Dunlop, R Burnett, R Dunlop

'King Joey shatters all records.' Despite slowing for the pits, his second lap is 0.4 seconds inside the outright lap record – on a 'mere' race-kitted RC30. With Hislop seizing on lap four, the winning margin from Nick Jefferies is 68 seconds.

Production Class C
1	B Morrison	CBR600 Honda	1:23:30.8	108.42mph*
11	**J Dunlop**	**CBR600 Honda**	**1:25:52.0**	**105.45mph(b)**

Record lap: S Hislop, Honda, 20:36.6, 109.83mph

Joey goes on another proddy cruise in a race contested at fearsome speed. The lap record is broken no less than 73 times.

Production Class B
1	S Hislop	Honda RC30	1:20:38.2	112.29mph*
5	**J Dunlop**	**Honda RC30**	**1:21:49.4**	**110.66mph**

Record lap: G Johnson, Bimota YB4, 20:02.2, 112.98mph

Joey's habitual caution in production events is overcome by the RC30's pedigree as he runs on the pace for the first time.

Production Class A
1	D Leach	FZR1000 Yamaha	1:19:12.2	114.32mph*

Record lap: G Johnson, FZR1000 Yamaha, 19:25.4, 116.55mph
J Dunlop: non-starter.

Junior 250cc
1	J Dunlop	249 Honda	1:20:56.6	111.87mph*

Record lap: S Hislop, Yamaha, 19:57.6, 113.41mph

Practice: 11th in Junior, almost 5mph slower than Brian Morrison, despite which Joey had predicted that 'Compared to last year the bike handles better and goes better. The lap record will be hammered.' And so it proved. However it's Hislop – 'the new pretender' according to Joey – who sets the new mark.

Senior
1	J Dunlop	750 Honda	1:15:42.6	117.38mph*

Record lap: S Cull, Honda, 19:00.6, 119.08mph

Joey's 13th win, by 50.6 seconds, is harder than it looked. A ferocious tussle with Steve Cull's ex-Joey 500 ends when the triple catches fire and burns out on the run down to Brandish. 'I knew Cull would give me a run. He's brave and quick and doesn't abuse the bikes.'

World Formula One Championship

Sugo, Japan, 15 May
1	N Miura	750 Honda	1:21:32.57	85.44mph

J Dunlop did not compete.

Isle of Man TT, 4 June: see TT results

Assen, Dutch TT, 23 June
1	R Burnett	750 Honda	58:51.07	97.15mph
8	**J Dunlop**	**750 Honda**		

Fastest lap: R Burnett, Honda, 2:18.47, 99.09mph

Vila Real, Portugal, 3 July
1	S Williams	750 Bimota	51:21.4	80.38mph
4	**J Dunlop**	**750 Honda**		

Fastest lap: J Dunlop, Honda, 2:44.4, 94.15mph

In Ireland a paddock is usually precisely that. This one's at Tandragee. (Stephen Davison – Pacemaker)

Joey draws deep on another tab at the 1994 TT. Quitting smoking a year later would help extend his competitive career. (Double Red)

After a disastrous pit stop, Joey could finish only sixth in the 1997 Formula One TT – but that didn't stop the fans cheering him on. (Phil Masters)

North-West 200, 250cc race 1997. Joey leads a group out of the 'new' chicane and back on to the seafront. (Phil Masters)

Kouvola, Finland, 17 July
1	A Andersson	750 Suzuki	1:16:04.88	77.60mph
3	**J Dunlop**	**750 Honda**		

Fastest lap: J Dunlop, Honda, 1:33.13, 79.39mph

Ulster Grand Prix, Dundrod, 30 July
1	C Fogarty	750 Honda	52:2.0	111.01mph
7	**J Dunlop**	**750 Honda**		

Fastest lap: C Fogarty, Honda, (time n/a), 116.10mph

Pergusa, Sicily, 4 September
1	C Fogarty	750 Honda	1:01:32.92	95.89mph

Fastest lap: n/a

J Dunlop DNF.

Donington Park, England, 25 September
1	N Mackenzie	750 Honda	1:07:49.75	88.45mph
11	**J Dunlop**	**750 Honda**		

Fastest lap: N Mackenzie, Honda, 1:39.74, 90.23mph

Joey suffers a torrid time in the most far-flung Formula 1 championship ever. A 'disaster' at Assen, last lap seizure in Finland, wrong tyre choice at Dundrod, and a big practice crash at Pergusa, all take their toll as Foggy claims the first of his world titles.

Final Championship Standings
1	C Fogarty	Honda	84
2	**J Dunlop**	**Honda**	**63½**
3	R Burnett	Honda	52

World Superbike Championship

Donington Park 3 April

Race 1
1	D Tardozzi	Bimota	
3	**J Dunlop**	**Honda**	

Race 2
1	M Lucchinelli	Ducati	
5	**J Dunlop**	**Honda**	

Hungary 30 April

Race 1
1	F Merkel	Honda	
6	**J Dunlop**	**Honda**	

Hockenheim 8 May

Race 1
1	D Tardozzi	Bimota	
7	**J Dunlop**	**Honda**	

Race 2
1	D Tardozzi	Bimota	
5	**J Dunlop**	**Honda**	

Joey dabbles with the inaugural WSB series, finishing 13th in the championship on 30 points. Fred Merkel wins on another Honda RC30.

North-West 200 wins
750cc Production

Ulster Grand Prix wins
350cc (race 1)

1989 TT

Joey enters no less than six TTs, but a serious crash at in the Eurolantic Series at Brands Hatch on Good Friday, 24 March, rules him out and effectively puts paid to his season. His main injuries are a broken thigh and wrist. At the TT prizegiving, Honda race boss Bob McMillan publicly promises him bikes for the TT for 'as long as he wants to race'. Carl Fogarty retains what would be the last Formula One World Championship, with Joey's brother Robert in third.

World Formula One Championship, Final Standings
1	C Fogarty	Honda	90
2	S Hislop	Honda	82
3	R Dunlop	Honda	54

Joey Dunlop did not contest the series due to injury.

1990 TT

Still handicapped by his Brands Hatch crash of Easter 1989, Joey is not the force he used to be around the TT circuit, although his enthusiasm appears undiminished. Practice is once again disrupted by weather, with Saturday's 'emergency' session used for the first time. Hislop dominates practice, but Fogarty takes an F1-Senior double.

Formula 1
1	C Fogarty	Honda RC30	1:554:45.6	118.53mph
8	**J Dunlop**	**Honda RC30**	**1:59:20.6**	**113.81mph**

Record lap: S Hislop, Honda RVF750, 18:27.6, 122.63mph
Team Award: Honda: C Fogarty, S Hislop, J Dunlop

Joey is delighted to finish his first TT for two years, and with a silver replica and team award: 'I tried hard to Ramsey on the first lap and got tired, so then settled for a finish.'

Ultra-Lightweight 125cc
1	R Dunlop	125 Honda	1:05:40.2	103.41mph*

Record lap: R Dunlop, 21:44.8, 104.09mph
Team Award: Honda: C Fogarty, S Hislop, J Dunlop

As Robert scores his second successive 125 win, Joey's bike dies at Kirkmichael on the last lap after a race-long dice with Ian Newton for second. So maybe he's not the has-been some pundits suggested.

Junior 250cc
1	I Lougher	250 Yamaha	1:18:37.6	115.16mph*

Record lap: I Lougher, Yamaha, 19:13.0, 117.80mph

The Junior is remarkable for a race-long dice between Lougher and Hislop, settled in the Welshman's favour by a mere 1.8 seconds. Joey retires at the pits with a misfire on lap four after lying 7th earlier in the race with a fastest lap of 113.68mph.

Senior
1	C Fogarty	Honda RC30	2:02:25.2	110.95mph
16	**J Dunlop**	**Honda RC30**	**2:11:48.8**	**103.04mph(b)**

Fastest lap: D Leach, Yamaha, 19:26.2, 116.47mph

On the opening lap of a rain-delayed race, Joey accidentally hits the kill button whilst wiping his visor on Cronk-y-Voddy straight: 'When I turned it on again it blew the exhaust clean off.' His pit crew spend several minutes fixing the problem, dropping him to 22nd before he clawed back to 16th. Hislop spent some time following the master: 'His line is still spot-on everywhere. He's magic to follow.'

FIM TT Formula One Cup

Sugo, Japan, 13 May
1	K Iwahashi	750 Honda	1:18:33.16	86.92mph

Fastest lap: S Miyazaki, Honda, 1:34.26, 88.69mph

Joey did not compete.

Isle of Man TT, 2 June: see TT results

Vila Real, Portugal, 1 July
1	C Fogarty	750 Honda	1:08:26.33	94.31mph
3	**J Dunlop**	**750 Honda**		

Fastest lap: C Fogarty | | | 2:39.33 | 97.225mph |

Kouvola, Finland, 15 July
1	C Fogarty	750 Honda	1:25:58.46	68.41mph
5	**J Dunlop**	**750 Honda**		

Fastest lap: C Fogarty, Honda, (not avail), (not avail)

Ulster Grand Prix, Dundrod, 11 August

1	J Dunlop	750 Honda	47:45.56	120.875mph

Record lap: J Dunlop, Honda, 3:36.73, 122.937mph

The Formula 1 series loses full World Championship status, although all rounds save Sugo are once again on street circuits. But with only Honda Britain contesting and Joey still not 100 per cent, Norton offer the only real opposition to Fogarty. The final round, at Dundrod, brings Joey his first international win since 1988, plus a new lap record. 'Just like the good old days' said Joey after a race-long tussle with Robert.

Final Championship standings
1	C Fogarty	71
2	**J Dunlop**	**54**
3	R Dunlop	49

1991 TT

The heyday of Hislop and Fogarty, riding the exotic factory Honda RVF750s, sees Joey again take a relative back seat. Robert Dunlop takes 125/250 double despite nursing a recently broken collarbone, with Joey second in each race.

Formula One
1	S Hislop	Honda RVF750	1:52:15.0	121.00mph

Record lap: S Hislop, Honda, 18:20.0, 123.48mph

Joey retires his RC30 at the pits with a blown fork seal when lying 21st at 113.26mph after lap one. Hislop wins by 1:16 from Foggy, both on exotic factory RVF750s.

Ultra-Lightweight 125cc
1	R Dunlop	125 Honda	1:27:19.8	103.68mph
2	**J Dunlop**	**125 Honda**	**1:27:59.2**	**102.91mph**

Fastest lap: R Dunlop, Honda, 21.12.8, 106.71mph
Team award: Honda: R Dunlop, J Dunlop, P McCallen

In damp conditions, Joey leads by 25 seconds at Glen Helen on lap two, but a fuel leak slows him after the pit stop. Robert acknowledges that 'It won't have helped my popularity to have stopped Joey equalling the record, but we're a competitive family.'

Junior 250cc
1	R Dunlop	Cowles Yamaha	1:18:48.8	114.89mph
5	**J Dunlop**	**Honda**	**1:20:47.8**	**112.07mph**

Fastest lap: P McCallen, Honda, 19:23.4, 116.75mph
Club Team Award: MCRRC of Ireland: R Dunlop, J Dunlop, J Rea

In a titanic battle in which every one of the top ten finishers averages over 110mph, Joey finishes a solid fifth despite a visor obscured by fuel and bugs. Brian Reid crashes heavily at Handleys.

Supersport 600
1	S Hislop	Honda CBR	1:19:14.2	114.28mph*
6	**J Dunlop**	**Honda CBR**	**1:20:37.2**	**112.31mph**

Record lap: S Hislop, 19:34.0, 115.69mph
Team Award: Honda: S Hislop, P McCallen, J Dunlop

Sixth is Joey's best TT result to date in a true production-based formula using road-legal tyres.

Senior
1	S Hislop	Honda RVF750	1:52:10.2	121.09mph
2	**J Dunlop**	**Honda RVF750**	**1:53.30.2**	**119.66mph**

Record lap: S Hislop, 18:21.8, 123.27mph
Team Award: Honda: S Hislop, J Dunlop, P McCallen,

Joey takes over the RVF used by Fogarty for the Formula One race, and crosses the finish line in formation with Hislop. At 119.66mph, his average speed is faster than his previous fastest lap and his fastest lap is a personal best at 121.51mph.

Ulster Grand Prix wins
Superbike (race 1)
Superbike (race 2)

1992 TT

At age 40 Joey finally nails that elusive record-equalling 14th TT win. In the larger classes Fogarty has left, but now Phillip McCallen – long tipped by Joey for TT stardom – shares the limelight with Hislop.

Formula One
1	P McCallen	Honda RC30	1:53:22.4	119.80mph
3	**J Dunlop**	**Honda RC30**	**1:55:13.0**	**117.88mph**

Fastest lap: Hislop 588 Norton, 18:21.6, 123.30mph
Team Award: Honda: P McCallen, J Dunlop, N Jefferies

McCallen wins when Foggy pulls out with gearbox problems. Just as in 1980, Joey struggles to hold the tank on with his knees when a bracket breaks at Quarter Bridge on lap two. 'It was similar to what happened in 1980, but I was a lot younger then. I had to ease off for all the jumps and bumps.'

Ultra-Lightweight 125cc
1	J Dunlop	Honda	1:25:01.6	106.49mph*

Record lap: J Dunlop, Honda, 20:49.6, 108.69mph

After trashing the lap record by 23 seconds, Joey admits that 'It's the first time I've raced hard here for years, but it's all worked out well.' Robert wryly suggests that 'Maybe he'll pack up now and give us all a chance.' Fat chance.

Supersport 600
1	P McCallen	Honda CBR	1:18:42.8	115.04mph*
9	**J Dunlop**	**Honda CBR**	**1:20:53.8**	**111.93mph**

Record lap: S Hislop, Honda, 19:20.8, 117.01mph
Team Award: Honda: P McCallen, S Hislop, J Dunlop

Joey: 'We hadn't really got the handling sorted out. It left a bit to be desired … and I'm a bit sore about the knees.'

Junior
1	B Reid	Yamaha	1:18:38.8	115.13mph

Fastest lap: S Hislop, Yamaha, 19:15.8, 117.51mph

Joey is lying fifth when he retires on lap three with a broken gearchange linkage.

Senior
1	S Hislop	Norton	1:51.59.6	121.28mph*

Record lap C Fogarty, Yamaha, 18:18.8, 123.61mph

On an emotional day for Norton, Joey, suffering from 'the lurgy' after two weeks of slimming for his 125cc effort, retires at the pits on lap three. 'It wasn't safe. I was seeing double at times. So I pulled out.' It's the first time he has retired from a TT for non-mechanical reasons.

Ulster Grand Prix wins
125cc

1993 TT

A second successive victory in the 125cc race puts Joey out his own with 15 TT wins. After the race he is mobbed, to chants of 'We love Joey'.

Formula One
1	N Jefferies	Honda RC30	1:54:57.2	118.15mph
14	**J Dunlop**	**Honda RC30**	**2:00:09.0**	**113.04mph(b)**

Fastest lap: M Farmer, Ducati, 18:46.4, 120.58mph

Joey complains that 'Something broke in the suspension. That's the worst TT I've ever had. Right from the start it was bad – OK on the corners, but I couldn't keep it in a straight line on the straights.'

Injuries sustained at Tandragee confined Joey to the smaller classes at the 1998 TT. Still in intense pain, he rounds the Bungalow in practice on the 250. (Phil Masters)

Surrounded by TT replicas at his display of memorabilia in 1998. (Stephen Davison – Pacemaker)

This old fella has kept generations of Douglas cub scouts running up and down the TT scoreboard for 25 years. (Stephen Davison – Pacemaker)

Even Himself doubted it could happen: Joey on his way to winning the Millennial Formula One TT. (Don Morley)

Ultra-Lightweight 125cc
| 1 | J Dunlop | Honda | 1:24:25.0 | 107.26mph* |

Fastest lap: J Dunlop, 20:51.2, 108.55mph

After claiming his 15th TT, Joey spoke emotionally of his 'incredible' reception on the last lap, 'way greater than last year when I equalled the record. I reckon every marshal on the course must have been waving.' Fittingly, his old sponsor John Rea was signalling for him at Windy Corner.

Supersport 600
| 1 | J Moodie | Honda CBR | 1:18:41.8 | 115.06mph* |

Fastest lap: J Moodie, Honda, 19:23.2, 116.77mph

Joey lies ninth place after lap one, but retires at Brandywell on lap two with handling problems.

Junior 250cc
| 1 | B Reid | Yamaha | 1:18:38.6 | 115.14mph |
| 3 | J Dunlop | Honda | 1:18:59.8 | 114.62mph |

Fastest lap: R Dunlop, Honda, 19:23.4, 116.75mph

In an Irish spectacular, Joey, Robert and Brian Reid spend part of the race battling on the road. Phillip McCallen throws away possible victory when he forgets to stop for fuel and runs out at Quarry Bends.

Senior
| 1 | P McCallen | Honda RC30 | 1:54:47.8 | 118.32mph |
| 11 | J Dunlop | Honda RC30 | 1:59:27.4 | 113.70mph |

Fastest lap: P McCallen, Honda, 18:45.8, 120.65mph

Joey lies second at half distance, 41 seconds behind McCallen, but later the Honda's breather bottle overflows. With the left side of the bike smothered with oil, he slips from sixth to 11th on the final lap.

Manx Grand Prix

Classic 350cc race
In his first Manx GP, Joey retires at the foot of Bray Hill on lap two when lying sixth.

1994 TT
An unhappy TT fortnight. Ireland's Mark Farmer is killed in practice at Black Dub. Then the postponed Formula One is blighted when Robert Dunlop's rear wheel collapses at Ballaugh. He undergoes nine hours of surgery to plate his right arm and right leg.

Formula One
| 1 | S Hislop | Honda RC45 | 1:53:37.2 | 119.54mph |
| 3 | J Dunlop | Honda RC45 | 1:56:23.61 | 116.69mph |

Fastest lap: P McCallen, Honda, 18:32.6, 122.08mph

The race is controversially abandoned after two laps due to rain and poor visibility on the Mountain. In Mad Sunday's re-run, a 'mortified' highway worker backs a tipper truck onto the course from his home near the 13th Milestone as Joey and Phil McCallen approach. Undaunted, the duo help Honda's new RC45 to a début 1-2-3.

Ultra-Lightweight 125cc
| 1 | J Dunlop | Honda | 1:25:38.0 | 105.74mph |

Fastest lap: J Dunlop, 21:04.6, 107.40mph

When early pace-setter Mick Lofthouse is black-flagged, Joey wins comfortably from Dennis McCullough. 'I won this one for him' said an emotional Joey of his injured brother Robert after the race. 'I just wish wee Robert had been out there racing with me.'

Supersport 600
| 1 | I Duffus | Yamaha | 1:18:32.0 | 115.30mph* |
| 7 | J Dunlop | Honda | 1:19:48.6 | 113.45mph |

Fastest lap: J Moodie, Yamaha, 19:23.8, 116.71mph

Joey spends the second half of the race in the company of Duffus and second-placed Ian Simpson. 'I was tired from the 125 race, but at least I know now that I can ride a 600 all right.'

Junior 250cc
| 1 | J Dunlop | Honda | 1:18:57.8 | 114.67mph |

Fastest lap: B Reid, Yamaha, 19:31.2, 115.97mph
Team Award: Honda: J Dunlop, I Simpson, I Lougher

Joey stalls on the line, but after that the luck runs his way when a footrest bolt falls out but the rest somehow stays in place. For the second successive year, McCallen runs out of fuel.

Senior
| 1 | S Hislop | Honda RC45 | 1:53:53.8 | 119.25mph |
| 3 | J Dunlop | Honda RC45 | 1:56:20.2 | 116.75mph |

Fastest lap: S Hislop, Honda, 18:28.8 112.50mph

A comfortable win for Hislop in another RC45 1-2-3. Joey is happy with 'my best TT week of racing for a long time, but I was tired out and just wanted to finish'. As if to prove just how tired, he wins each of the three races he enters at the post-TT Steam Packet races. In total he would score no less than 40 wins on the Billown Circuit: 29 in the Southern 100, 11 in Steam Packet post-TT races.

Ulster Grand Prix wins
125cc
Superbike race 1

Manx Grand Prix

Classic 350cc race
Riding an Aermacchi again, Joey places second in his last MGP appearance.

1995 TT
Just as people are writing Joey off as a lightweight specialist, up he pops and wins the Senior for the first time since before his big Brands Hatch crash in 1989. Yet typically, he'd stood only a lowly 11th in the F1/Senior practice rankings. After he complained of a slide at the Verandah during practice, council workmen removed the shiny white lines there.

Formula One
| 1 | P McCallen | Honda RC45 | 1:55:15.8 | 117.84mph |
| 2 | J Dunlop | Honda RC45 | 1:55:33.9 | 117.53mph |

Fastest lap: P McCallen, Honda, 18:43.9, 120.85mph

Joey tantalisingly takes the lead by just one second when McCallen changes helmets at the end of lap two, but loses time to fix loose ram-air ducts which were costing the motor 1000rpm. McCallen wins despite a loose rear wheel.

Ultra-Lightweight 125cc
| 1 | M Baldwin | Honda | 1:24:30.8 | 107.14mph |

Record lap: M Baldwin, Honda, 20:46.0, 109.01mph

Having been second in practice, Joey seizes at Hawthorn on lap one. Mick Lofthouse is second by 0.6 seconds after leading almost the entire race.

Lightweight 250cc
| 1 | J Dunlop | Honda | 1:18:16.4 | 115.68mph* |

Fastest lap: J Dunlop, Honda, 19:15.2, 117.57mph
Team Award: Honda: J Dunlop, J Courtney, P McCallen
Club Award: MCRRC of Ireland: J Dunlop, J Courtney, D McCullough

Ten years after his first 250 win, Joey claims another, by 24.5 seconds from James Courtney, taking 21 seconds off Ian Lougher's five-year race record. 'I was half expecting the bike to seize like the 125 did this morning. It took me to Glen Helen to put that out of my mind. The bike never missed a beat. It was one of the best rides I've had around here.'

Junior
1	I Duffus	Honda CBR	1:17:40.4	116.58mph*
4	**J Dunlop**	**Honda CBR**	**1:19:01.6**	**114.58mph**

Record lap: I Duffus, Honda, 19:12.3, 117.87mph

In a keenly fought 600 race (now called the 'Junior' TT), places two to five are covered by less than 0.5mph. This is Joey's best 'proddy-bike' performance at the TT in 'trouble-free' ride on the CBR600 Honda

Senior
1	**J Dunlop**	**Honda RC45**	**1:54:01.9**	**119.11mph**

Fastest lap: S Ward, Honda, 18:35.8, 121.73mph
Team Award: Honda: J Dunlop, S Ward, N Jefferies

'Dazzling Dunlop' takes the win by over 30 seconds from Iain Duffus who reports that he 'only had one problem: Joey Dunlop.' Joey says: 'That was hard work, after the two strokes – this race is two laps longer and the bike twice the weight.'

Ulster Grand Prix wins
250cc (race 1)
250cc (race 2)
Superbike (race 1)

1996 TT

Non-smoker Joey comes of age with wins 20 and 21, but his practice form typically gives little hint of the success to come. It's another bleak practice week as Mick Lofthouse and Robert Holden are killed in the same practice session, in a fortnight that also claims two other riders.

Formula One
1	P McCallen	Honda RC45	1:56:54.1	116.18mph
7	**J Dunlop**	**Honda RC45**	**1:59:53.4**	**113.29mph**

Fastest lap: I Duffus, 750 Honda, 18:44.0, 120.84mph
Club Team Award: MCRRC of Ireland: P McCallen, J Dunlop, D Young

Joey's chances in an incident-packed race are lost in the pits. When he charges in to change from intermediate to slick after lap one, no wheel is ready, he has to go out, then pit again after lap two.

Lightweight 250cc
1	**J Dunlop**	**Honda RC250R**	**1:18:31.5**	**115.31mph**

Fastest lap: P McCallen, Honda, 19:24.5, 116.94mph
Team Award: Honda: J Dunlop, J Moodie, J Griffiths
Club Team Award: MCRRC of Ireland: J Dunlop, D Young, D McCullough

In a thrilling race, McCallen leads by a mere 1.9 seconds after two laps, but a slow pit stop puts Joey ahead. When McCallen holes an exhaust in pursuit, late-charging Jim Moodie harries Joey home as he struggles to make his fuel last the distance.

Ultra-Lightweight 125cc
1	**J Dunlop**	**125 Honda**	**42:34.6**	**106.33mph**

Fastest lap: J Dunlop, Honda, 21:02.1, 107.62mph
Team award: Honda: J Dunlop, G Lee, G English

In a two lap race, Joey and Gavin Lee reach Ramsey Hairpin neck-and-neck the second time around, but the master's trackcraft pays off as he forges a 3.8 second advantage through treacherous banks of mist on the Mountain to set the fastest lap of the race.

Senior
1	P McCallen	Honda RC45	1:53:24.8	119.76mph
2	**J Dunlop**	**Honda RC45**	**1:54:37.2**	**118.50mph**

Fastest lap: P McCallen, Honda, 18:32.0, 122.14mph
Team Award: Honda: P McCallen, J Dunlop, N Jefferies

McCallen leads from start to finish in yet another RC45 1-2-3, with Nick Jefferies in third and the challenge from Jim Moodie's Kawasaki expiring with a broken plug lead after four laps.

1997 TT

In superb weather, Joey takes his 22nd win and team-mate McCallen grabs three wins in a week which is emphatically Honda's. Of 60 top-ten places in the major solo events, Big Aitch take no less than 44.

Formula One
1	P McCallen	Honda RC45	1:53:16.8	119.90mph
6	**J Dunlop**	**Honda RC45**	**1:56:29.4**	**116.60mph**

Fastest lap: McCallen, Honda, 18:24.4, 122.98mph

After a fast start, Joey's challenge evaporates when his rear wheel nut jams at the first pit stop costing him 70 seconds and dropping him from the leaderboard. 'The same thing happened to me last year. This year we were supposed to have a new system, but it didn't work.'

Lightweight 250cc
1	**J Dunlop**	**Honda**	**1:18:20.1**	**115.59mph**

Fastest lap: J McGuinness, Aprilia, 19:22.6, 116.83mph
Team Award: Honda: J Dunlop, I Lougher, G Dynes

Joey is pushed hard by McCallen, who changes the rear wheel at half distance and crashes out at Quarry Bends trying to recover time. Joey doesn't change wheels, and despite a sliding rear tyre, comfortably holds Lougher at bay in a win reminiscent of his heyday.

Ultra-Lightweight 125cc
1	I Lougher	Honda	1:23:55.4	107.89mph
10	**J Dunlop**	**Honda**	**1:26:20.7**	**104.87mph(b)**

Record lap: I Lougher, Honda, 20:43.2, 109.25mph

Pre-race favourite Joey struggles with a bike which is down on top speed to finish a disappointing tenth. Riding Patsy O'Kane's Honda, Robert scores an emotional third place after his career-threatening injuries in 1994.

Junior 600cc
1	I Simpson	Honda CBR	1:16:28.3	118.41mph*
5	**J Dunlop**	**Harris Honda**	**1:17:42.6**	**116.52mph**

Record lap: I Simpson, Honda, 18:53.2, 119.86mph

The hottest news is Simmo's sensational record, only a fraction off 120mph. But Joey is genuinely mixing it with the young pretenders and 'enjoyed the race, but got confused between the 600 and 125 because I out braked myself going into Braddan on the first lap.'

Senior
1	P McCallen	Honda RC45	1:53:36.6	119.55mph
7	**J Dunlop**	**Honda RC45**	**1:56:01.3**	**117.07mph**

Fastest lap: P McCallen, 18:31.5, 122.22mph

Expectations were high of the NSR500 V-twins ridden in practice by Joey and Jim Moodie, but at the last minute Joey elects to ride the 750. In the race he loses out to an enthralling tussle between McCallen, Moodie, Rutter, Beck, Jackson and Simpson.

Ulster Grand Prix wins
250cc (race 2)

1998 TT

Honda's 50th birthday party gets off to a poor start when Joey breaks his left hand and collarbone, cracks his pelvis and loses part of a finger crashing out of the Tandragee 100 races early in May. He's too sore to ride the F1 race. McCallen sits out the entire TT after crashing at Thruxton. And the weather is truly appalling. The silver lining is Honda's 100th TT win.

Lightweight 250cc
1	**J Dunlop**	**Honda RS250**	**46:51.8**	**96.61mph**

Fastest lap: J Dunlop, Honda, 22:31.4, 100.50mph
Team Award: Honda: J Dunlop, J McGuinness, J Courtney

Although too sore to ride the F1 bike, riding Callum Ramsey's kitted RS250, Joey certainly knew how to out-fox his opponents. In ominous weather, most of the field pits after lap one. Joey doesn't, and when the race is shortened to two laps, needs no pit stop at all. But victory is his by 43.1 seconds, so he'd probably have won, anyway.

The North-West 200 showed that the kitted SP-1 couldn't cut it for top speed. Something faster was needed. (Stephen Davison – Pacemaker)

Joey's gloves on the F1 bike, 2000: the left one absolutely had to go on first. (Stephen Davison – Pacemaker)

Those two brothers at it again. Joey and Robert dicing at Aghadowey for the final time. (Stephen Davison – Pacemaker)

Ultra-Lightweight 125cc

1	R Dunlop	O'Kane Honda 125	1:03:50.3	106.38mph
9	**J Dunlop**	**McMenemy Honda 125**	**1:06:25.8**	**102.23mph**

Fastest lap: I Lougher, 21:03.1, 107.53mph
Club award: MCRCC of Ireland: R Dunlop, G Dynes, J Dunlop

Possibly Joey's most satisfying defeat, as battered brother Robert wins, despite hobbling to his Honda on crutches with a half-healed broken shin and collarbone. 'When I was lying in the road at the North-West 200,' says Robert, 'I didn't think I'd be riding here.'

Senior

1	I Simpson	Honda Britain RC45	1:53:23.1	119.79mph

Fastest lap: M Rutter, Honda, 18:23.9, 123.04mph

J Dunlop retires at the pits after lap three, before vowing that 'I'll be back to win another title.'

1999 TT

In a strange TT, not a single Irishman wins a race for the first time since 1981, and a Honda fails to win the Formula One event for the first time since the same year. But the outright lap record finally goes. Tragically, Joey's Honda team-mate Simon Beck is killed at the 33rd Milestone in practice.

Formula 1

1	D Jefferies	Yamaha R1	1:14:37.0	121.35mph
2	**J Dunlop**	**Honda RC45**	**1:14:52.8**	**120.92mph**

Fastest lap: D Jefferies, 18:21.9, 123.26mph

In a race restarted after Paul Orritt crashes on Bray Hill, Joey pushes Jefferies all the way despite changing a near-shredded Michelin after four laps. Trailing by 14 seconds with one lap to go, Joey charges to his fastest-ever TT lap at 123.06mph, but Jefferies goes quicker still.

Lightweight 250cc

1	J McGuinness	Honda 250	1:17:31.7	116.79mph
5	**J Dunlop**	**Payne Honda RS250**	**1:19:05.8**	**114.48mph**

Record lap: J McGuinness, 19:08.2, 118.29mph
Team Award: Honda: J McGuinness, D McCullough, J Dunlop

Joey's defence of the title he'd won for the previous five years is foiled when James Courtney crashes in front of him at Greeba Castle. Luckily Courtney's injuries are not serious, but Joey is de-tuned. The winner was aged three when Joey won his first TT.

Ultra-Lightweight 125cc

1	I Lougher	Honda RS125	1:24:17.3	107.43mph
27	**J Dunlop**	**McMenemy Honda 125**	**1:33:26.1**	**96.91mph (no replica)**

Fastest lap: J Dunlop, 20:44.7, 109.12mph

Fourth in practice, Joey stops to make adjustments at Ballacraine and loses more time clearing a blocked fuel breather in the pits. He goes on to set the fastest lap of the race at 109.22mph, just 1.5 seconds outside the lap record, yet fails even to earn a bronze replica.

Junior 600cc

1	J Moodie	Honda CBR	1:16:39.8	118.11mph
5	**J Dunlop**	**Harris Honda CBR600**	**1:17:13.3**	**117.26mph**

Fastest lap: D Jefferies, 18:53.6, 119.82mph
Team Award: Honda: J Moodie, J Dunlop, A Archibald

Senior

1	D Jefferies	V&M Yamaha R1	1:51:59.8	121.27mph
5	**J Dunlop**	**Honda RC45**	**1:53:28.5**	**119.69mph**

Record lap: J Moodie, 18:11.4, 124.45mph

Joey Dunlop came home fifth before pronouncing that the RC45's days were over.

Ulster Grand Prix wins
Superbike (race 2)

2000 TT

Formula 1

1	**J Dunlop**	**Honda VTR SP-1**	**1:52:15.3**	**120.99mph***

Fastest lap: D Jefferies, 1000 Yamaha, 18:22.6, 123.18mph
Team award: Honda: J Dunlop, J McGuinness, J Moodie

Using Aaron Slight's WSB engine and with Honda president Mr Kawashima looking on, even Joey admits to feeling under pressure. But on a daunting mixture of wet and dry road, he's in a class of his own once Jefferies' Yamaha breaks down, and wins comfortably from Michael Rutter. Joey's average race speed is the fastest he would ever record. He's mobbed in delirious scenes at the finish.

Lightweight 250cc

1	**J Dunlop**	**Payne Honda RS250**	**58:32.2**	**116.01mph**

Fastest lap: J Dunlop, 19:25.4, 116.55mph
Team Award: Honda: J Dunlop, I Lougher, S Harris

Although rain delays the race by several hours and reduces it from four laps to three, nothing can dampen the passion of the crowds as the King of the Roads posts a barely credible quarter century of TT wins. 'That was the best I've ever ridden The Island on a 250,' he pronounces. 'I had a lot of trouble setting up the machine in practice but it ran like a dream today.'

Ultra-Lightweight 125cc

1	**J Dunlop**	**Honda RS125**	**1:24:30.8**	**107.14mph**

Fastest lap: J Dunlop, 20:51.1, 108.56mph
Team Award: Honda: J Dunlop, D McCullough, R Dunlop

Victory gives Joey three wins in a week for the third time in his career – itself, inevitably, a record. In an Ulster clean sweep, Dennis McCullough places second, with Robert Dunlop third. Having led from flag to flag, Joey says afterwards that 'As soon as I got down Bray Hill on the first lap I knew the machine was going well. That gave me the heart to go for the win.'

Junior

1	D Jefferies	Yamaha R6	1:15:52.8	119.33mph
4	**J Dunlop**	**Harris Honda CBR600**	**1:16:26.7**	**118.45mph**

Record lap: A Archibald, 600 Honda, 18:41.1, 121.15mph

In a race run at searing pace by men half his age, Joey places an impressive fourth in a class in which he has rarely excelled, despite admitting to being 'worn out' by his exploits in the 125cc race a few hours earlier.

Senior

1	D Jefferies	V&M Yamaha R1	1:51:22.8	121.95mph
3	**J Dunlop**	**Honda VTR SP-1**	**1:52:33.8**	**120.66mph**

Record lap: D Jefferies, 18:00.6, 125.69mph

Jefferies leads throughout in a race postponed to Saturday although Joey, ever the mercurial starter, ties for the lead at Glen Helen on lap one. From there he 'gave it everything but it's been a long hard week ... I was just too tired to attack.' On his sixth lap Joey has the satisfaction of posting a time of 18:16.5/123.87mph, in what proves to be his last and fastest-ever lap of the TT Mountain circuit.

Index